British Railways Illustrated
SUMMER SPECIAL
No.3

SEASIDE BANK HOLIDAY ARRANGEMENTS

Beach Attendant from Prom. : ''Yer'll have to move 'em all up a bit Stanley, 'eres *another* train in.''

IRWELL
PRESS

CONTENTS

SUBSCRIPTIONS

Readers can subscribe for six or twelve issues at a time. The cost for six issues is £13.20 inclusive of postage and packing whilst twelve issues are charged at £26.40. Overseas subscribers should add the cost of surface/air mail. Limited numbers of back issues are also available. All remittances should be made out to IRWELL PRESS MAGAZINES LTD and sent to :-

The General Manager's Office,
P.O.Box 1260, Caernarfon,
Gwynedd, LL55 3ZD
Telephone : 01286 871776
Fax : 01286 871605

EDITORIAL MATTERS

Contributions, submissions, photographs or whatever (remember the contributor must address and attend to copyright), readers' letters, bouquets and brickbats to Editor, Chris Hawkins at 3, Durley Avenue, Pinner, Middlesex HA5 1JQ. Tel:0181 868 3230; FAX:0181 866 6915

Photo right :- English seaside mud. The 1.54pm Gravesend Central - Allhallows on Sea picks its way under a giant sky with H tank 31005 on 18th April 1960. J.J.Smith.

Photo left :- BR 4-6-0 No.73114 leaves Wimbledon Yard with a down freight, 9th March 1964. P. Lynch.

Cartoon - from LMS Magazine, August 1934.

ISBN 1-817608-72-4

Welcome to the third **British Railways Illustrated Summer Special.** It's less buckets and spades this year and more of a trip to the countryside and the great outdoors, more *Health and Efficiency* if you like than *Kiss Me Quick.* Strawberries have always spelt summer for some reason in this country: the Wimbledon connection is obvious but it probably has more to do with folk memory - the fruit's long established 'unobtainable - unaffordable' status that anyone treated to the things (heaped in white sugar of course) a lifetime away in 1956 will never quite forget. All this is a rather laboured effort to establish the strawberry's summer credentials and more deeply rooted summer memories might flow from a West Country branch line story - **The Strawberry Line** was an astonishing near-32 miles of rural branch threading across some of the best bits of Somerset; it accommodated tourist traffic but was principally there for the locals, playing an important role all year round in the economy of the district, with its quarries and, oh yes - exotic fruit.

The Isle of Wight was definitely bucket and spade territory though certainly it was slightly posher than, say, Hayling Island or Southsea - though maybe Bognor Regis or Bournemouth might compare socially. They all shared the South Coast perennials, 'The Front', ferocious landladies, postcards and candy floss, but a stay on the Island meant that extra little bit of adventure - that sea crossing, the Pier Head and rattling trains and locos. Many visitors could remain convinced throughout their week or fortnight that the trains were part of the Olde Worlde show put on by the Council. If only it were true. **Ticket to Ryde** is both a railway story and the tale of an enduring British institution, The Pier.

Wellingborough engine shed might not seem much of a holiday subject but in the 'fifties and 'sixties there was glorious countryside, well, *nice* countryside close by and what better for a school holiday afternoon than to sit and watch endless pounding freight trains? **A Personal View of 15A** is a collection of photographs from a local lad, one of the gallant few who managed to combine, far sightedly, his railway observations with picture taking.

Holidays in the Highlands of Scotland, in the 'fifties at least, were on rather a different social plane from the mud of the south coast. There was of course staggering scenery, and the adventure of getting there put even the poor old Pier Head in the shade a bit. It was certainly a place for summer visits, and West Highland photographs in this year's edition give a flavour of a wonderful piece of railway - one or two winter portraits indicate just *why* a summertime visit was preferable... Well into a second week at Bognor, it was easy to find one's mind wandering to those gaunt hillsides. **The Stuff of Legend** is an account put together largely from contemporary technical reports, describing some of the extraordinary effort that went into building the West Highland. *'On the moor of Rannoch for instance where the line will require special attention, there is not a house to be seen for miles ...'*

For those readers unfamiliar with the monthly magazine from which this *Summer Special* is spawned, there are a number of features which figure regularly and some of these always decorate both the *Summer Special* and the *Christmas Annual.* **Fourum** is an old favourite known to all, so is **Diesel Dawn** and **War Report. Thirties File** is another and for the purposes of our summer hols what could be better than **Building the Cornish Riviera Express?**

Marvellous postcard view, printed for sale to holidaymakers under the hopeful moniker *Sunray*. It is not recorded whether the purchasers' inevitable disgruntlement at writing such a card, rain dripping against the 'caff' window and the boarding house firmly barred for hours yet, was an ingredient in the demise of the *Sunray* series. Shows perfectly the conjunction of 'old' and 'new' piers - the former on right, with promenade section, latter to the left.

TICKET to RYDE

By Kevin Pile

The pier, was - and still is - an integral part of the traditional British holiday. At a handful of resorts railway enthusiasts could combine their summer break with an inspection of pier railways, and one of the best known was that at Ryde, on the Isle of Wight. This famous railway pier has provided literally millions of holidaymakers with their first toehold on the island - the pier was, however, not the first at Ryde, nor was the resort the first one to accommodate a railway. A little pre-history is in order. As explained by Don Bradley in his book *A Locomotive History of Railways on the Isle of Wight* (RCTS, 1982) the first pier opened in May 1814. With a length of 1,740ft (later extended to over 2,000ft) it was intended for use in conjunction with the Southsea - Ryde steamer services, but presented a rather long walk for passengers and, consequently, failed

0-4-4T No.211 (later SHANKLIN) leaves the pier, probably soon after its arrival in 1923 . Photograph BAJT.

No.27 MERSTONE runs along the pier with a Cowes train. The delicate, open tracery of the construction is seen to good effect, and it is hardly surprising that prolonged repairs were necessary at intervals over the years. Photograph BAJT.

to attract traffic away from the rival Southampton - Cowes service. Cowes had the distinct advantage in that the station was fairly close to the landing quay - a major benefit for passengers with heavy luggage. The advantages of Cowes were not wasted on the mainland railway companies. The LB&SCR introduced London - Cowes excursions

in 1859, the seaborne section being to and from Portsmouth, and the L&SWR soon followed suit.

Nothing was done to improve the facilities at Ryde Pier until 1862 when, spurred on by the Isle of Wight Railway's proposals for the Ryde - Ventnor line, the Pier company started work on an adjacent structure (built by John

Langdon) which was strong enough to carry a double-track tramway. The new pier opened to the public in March 1864, the *Isle of Wight Times* of 17 March 1864 commenting that: *'This is a vast improvement on the old system, which should curb the dissatisfaction apparent at present'*. In August 1871 matters were further improved when

A crowded Pier Head. To the visitor making a slightly tottering progress 'down the plank' from the paddle steamer there was nevertheless an air of efficiency, despite the wheezing ancientry of these strange trains; a sea of cases had to be negotiated and if the sun was shining it could add up to a quite heady holiday expectation of goodies to come - especially as the sudden shelter of the station sharply increased the warmth of what sun there might be.

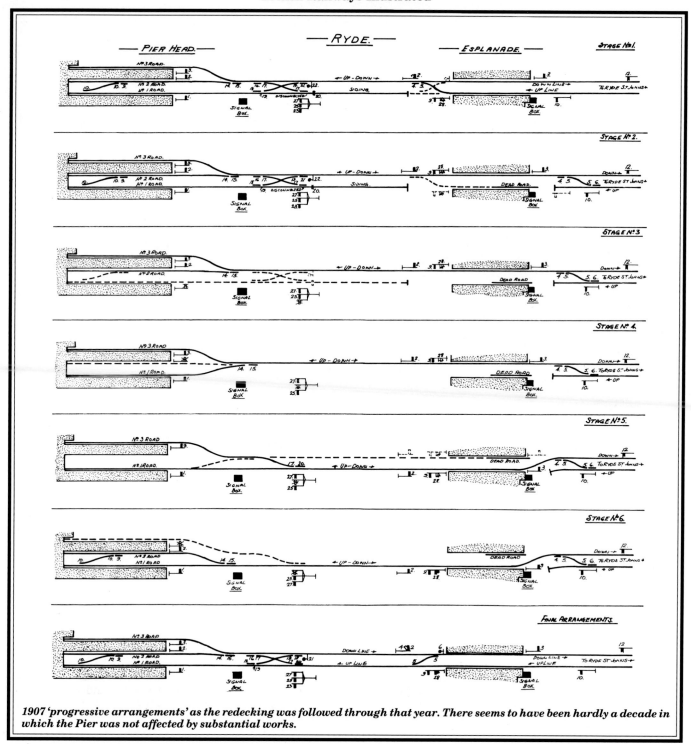

1907 'progressive arrangements' as the redecking was followed through that year. There seems to have been hardly a decade in which the Pier was not affected by substantial works.

the tramway was extended to St.John's Road station, thus making a useful connection between the steamers and the Isle of Wight Railway, although many locals considered that the new works spoiled the beach.

Initially, trains on the pier were horse-worked, earlier trials with a small Manning Wardle 0-4-0ST named *Vectis* having caused the pier to vibrate alarmingly. In 1868 thoughts were given to replacing the horses with a stationary steam engine, but that notion came to nothing. In 1876 attempts to employ a steam tram engine were vetoed by the Board of Trade, but a pair of gas-fired steam carriages was nevertheless employed between 1881 and 1884. After a two-year hiatus, during which horse-power was again used,

electric traction took over in April 1886. By then the pier and its tramway was facing stiff competition.

The New Pier
Let's go back to 1877. The LSWR and LBSCR viewed with interest the expanding traffic to and from the Isle of Wight, and considered that the original pier and its (then) horse-worked tramway fell a long way short of meeting potential demands. The two mainland companies therefore jointly promoted a bill for the construction of a completely new pier at Ryde, served by a double-track railway from St.John's Road station. Although some locals questioned the wisdom of permitting the two 'big boys from across the water' to gain such an ingress to

the island, the bill passed the Parliamentary stages unopposed, and gained Royal Assent in July 1877.

The joint LSWR/LBSCR line at Ryde was only 1 mile 19 chains in length, but with much of it over waves, it will immediately be appreciated that it involved considerable engineering work. A substantial pier had to be constructed, and also a tunnel for part of the way between the Esplanade and St.John's Road station. In later years, flooding of the tunnel was a not-infrequent occurrence; embarrassingly, the railway-owned *Esplanade Hotel* at Ryde was also prone to a watery basement.

Apart from some delay with the pier piling, construction proceeded rapidly. As an interim measure, only a single

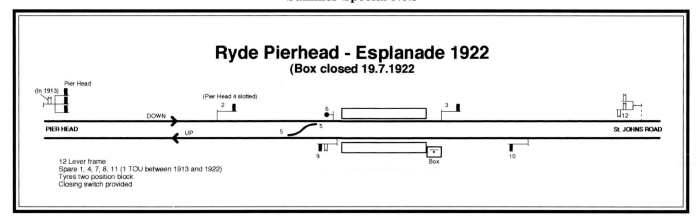

Ryde Pierhead - Esplanade 1922
(Box closed 19.7.1922

PIER HEAD   St. JOHNS ROAD

12 Lever frame
Spare 1, 4, 7, 8, 11 (1 TOU between 1913 and 1922)
Tyres two position block
Closing switch provided

Ryde Pier Head station, 21 April 1957. The structure on the right is the station signal box, while the tracks in the foreground are those of the old pier tramway of 1864. Just about discernible are an O2 at Platform Three of Pier Head station, and one of the tramway's Drewry cars (extreme left). Photograph Derek Clayton.

Ryde Pier Head signal box, 21 April 1957. The old tramway pier is in the foreground. Photograph Derek Clayton.

line of rails was laid between St.John's Road station and the Esplanade (or the Pier Gates, as it was known) and the works were inspected by Colonel Yolland for the Board of Trade on 20 February 1880.

The report included the obligatory description...'a ruling gradient of 1 in 50 (rising towards Esplanade station) ...sharpest curve 8 chains (with check rails) ...double-headed rails weighing 82lb to the yard ...transverse sleepers

of creosoted Baltic timber ...laid on ballast of beach gravel one-foot thick'.

Col. Yolland observed a few minor blemishes - 'slight appearances of settlement' in the brickwork of the viaducts carrying the road over the railway at St.John's Road, and also in a wing wall of the brickwork for the approach to the occupation road. There was already a tradition of petty squabbling between the railway companies and the councils (it continued through to very recent times) and the Colonel duly noted that 'A question' had arisen between 'the Corporation of Ryde and the Railway Companies' as to a short length of fencing alongside the approach road to the slipway, 'by which cattle, sheep and pigs coming on to the island are landed'. Nevertheless, permission to open the single line was granted, but subject to the completion of a bridge to carry Park Road across the railway. The temporary level crossing at that point did not find favour at all.

The single-track line between St.John's Road and the Pier Gates (Esplanade) opened on 5 April 1880, the services being worked by the Isle of Wight Railway. The second line of rails was inspected the following month, Colonel Yolland noting that, at Esplanade station the up and down platforms were 2ft 6in in height 'with a subway as a means of communication'. The signal box at the south end of the up platform had a locking frame containing twelve levers, one of them spare. The Colonel, however, could not sanction the opening of the line because 'the arrangements for connecting the double line with the Isle of Wight and Newport & Ryde (sic) Railways at St.John's Road station' were '...not satisfactory'.

It was hoped to have the Ryde Pier section ready in time for Whitsun, but bad weather hindered operations. The work was inspected by Colonel Yolland on 8 July 1880, his report including an interesting description of the pier itself:

'The railway is double throughout. It is entirely on a Viaduct [a novel way of describing a pier!] consisting of 12 spans of 40 feet and 43 spans of 20 feet.

'The 40-feet spans are covered by wrought iron girders, two for each line

'Spending the afternoon over here', says the message from John on the rear of this postcard which was mailed to a Miss Munro at Largs on 4 September 1913. In this view, the original pier and tramway are to the immediate left of the promenade section, the joint LBSC/LSW pier of 1880 the 'new' railway part being behind the tramway pier (the other side of the railings).

that No.2 lever that moves a down starting signal should not be used for two different roads.

'There are 3 lines at the Pier Head with 2 platforms, one of them an island platform ...The Station Buildings are at right angles to the line of railway.

'In bad weather the pier is an exposed place, and it would be a great convenience and comfort to the public embarking and disembarking from the Steam Boats if the two railway companies were to provide shelter from the tops of two or three of the landing places to the Station Buildings'.

Due mainly to the unfinished state of the island platform and the easternmost line, Col Yolland was prepared to 'pass' only two of the tracks and the western platform. That, however, was adequate for the present purpose, and public traffic commenced on 12 July 1880. The IWR retained a monopoly of pier workings until 4 October, when

View of the pier looking from the Esplanade, taken in March 1952 prior to the cleaning of the metalwork. The extent of the facilities at the Pier Head is very evident.

of Railway, supported on columns or piles of wrought iron known as Hughes piles, filled with concrete and driven to a depth of about 30 feet into the ground. These piles are stated to have been tested by having 50 tons of dead weight placed over each pile.

'The 20-feet spans, also crossed by wrought iron girders, are supported by cast iron screw piles each with 3 blades with wrought iron top length partly filled with concrete.

'There is a hand rail outside the outer girders, but I have suggested that wooden baulks should be securely bolted to the top of the two outer girders, one on each side, so as to form a guard rail to prevent any vehicle that may happen to get off the rails from any cause from falling over the edge of the Viaduct.

'The Pier Head Signal Box contains 28 levers, of which 4 are at present spare ones. The interlocking is correct, except

Esplanade station at Ryde, 21 April 1957. An unidentified O2 waits with a train for the Pier Head. The old pier and tramway are in the foreground. Photograph Derek Clayton.

O2 No 20 SHANKLIN takes on water at Platform Two, Pier Head. The year is 1953. The engine started life as LSWR No 211 in 1892, and in May 1923 it became one of the first pair of O2s to be transferred to the Isle of Wight. Prior to being shipped, it had its vacuum ejectors removed and replaced by Westinghouse gear, the island's railways having, by then, adopted air brakes as standard. The engine retained its LSWR livery and number until 1924, when it was painted Maunsell green and was given its new number at Ryde Works. The engine remained on the island for the rest of its life, and was withdrawn when steam haulage ceased at the end of 1966. Photograph Locofotos.

No.21 SANDOWN on the 11.25am Pier Head to Ventnor, arriving at Esplanade on 7th July 1955. Photograph Philip J. Kelley.

they were shared with the Ryde & Newport (later Isle of Wight Central) Railway.

Permission to open the third line and additional platform on the pier was given on 16 September but, during his inspection, Colonel Yolland commented on the railings alongside the railway at the Esplanade station: *'The original contract for the execution of the works... provided for a wall 4 feet 6 inches in height, but at the request of the Town Council the Railway Companies constructing the line agreed to substitute a substantial iron railing fixed on a low wall so that the view from the road and houses on the south side of the Esplanade should not be interfered with.*

'No fencing that could reasonably be asked for will prevent boys from clambering over it, as in the short time I was on the Esplanade I observed a boy getting OVER the top of the iron railing at a point where the railings were no less than 7 feet from the ground'.

The matter of the railings had been brought to Colonel Yolland's attention by the Town Council. In the various BoT reports, it is conspicuous how frequently council representatives (including, on at least one occasion, the Mayor) urged the Colonel to demand that the railway companies do this, that, and the other.

Inevitably, the new pier attracted a significant proportion of the traffic to and from the mainland. There was, of course, the long-standing rival port of entry at Cowes, but another potential rival surfaced in 1885. In August of that year, a ferry service was introduced between Langstone Harbour and St.Helens, the latter point being served by the IWR's Bembridge branch, which had opened in 1882. The new service was worked by a vessel by the name of *Carrier*, which had previously operated between Granton and Burntisland in Scotland, but it lasted only until March 1888. The fortunes of the old (1864) pier at Ryde

Fine show in grim weather - No.31 CHALE between Pier Head and Esplanade with the 12.27pm to Ventnor, 28th December 1965. Photograph Phil Lynch.

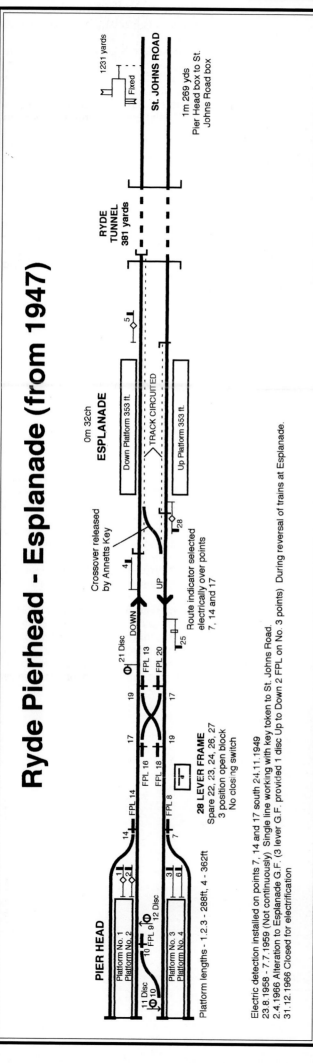

Ryde Pierhead - Esplanade (from 1947)

declined, although not to the extent that might be imagined. Nevertheless, with the opening of the new railway pier in 1880, the trams on the old pier ceased operating through to St.John's Road station. Latterly, the tram fares between the pier head and the station had been 10d (first class) and 5d (second class). Perhaps surprisingly, though, the trams continued operating along the pier for many years, more of which anon.

The Joint Committee

Ryde Pier was administered by a joint LSWR/ LBSCR committee, The venue for the meetings usually alternated between Waterloo and London Bridge stations but, very occasionally, meetings were held at Portsmouth. A full set of the joint committee's minutes survives at the Public Record Office (RAIL 411/ 284) and the varied pontifications referring to Ryde and the pier capture something of the parochial atmosphere.... The Committee, on hearing the Engineer's recommendation to the General Managers, agreed on 5 January 1892 for instance that 'an Apparatus for heating footwarmers' be provided, at a cost of £13. A new crane was ordered for Ryde Esplanade on 8 January 1895, or rather a spare secondhand example, whilst in July 1899 Messrs. Pickford & Co paid

the sum of £34.4s.0d, 'being a moiety of the cost of repairing the damage done by their vessel "Midge" to the Pier on 6 February last'. The same year, some dredging on the east side of the Pier 'for the better mooring of the Joint Committee's Steamers' was arranged, at an estimated cost of £75, a Mr.Frank Bevis of Portsmouth having offered to do the work at 2s.4d per cubic yard. Enlargement of the Parcels Office at the Esplanade station was authorised, as well as a further alteration of the General Waiting Room, at a total estimated cost of £25. It was a difficult year: a Mr Sweetman had to pay £2.1s.7d, 'being one-half the cost of repairing the damage done to the gates by his runaway horse'.

The Minutes for 1906 reveal that in July 'reinforced concrete decking in place of the present timber decking on the Pier' was under discussion. The work was duly entrusted to Messrs. John Cochrane & Sons of 39 Victoria Street, Westminster, at the price of 13s.6d per square yard. 'The price was quoted' the Minutes record, 'on the understanding that the work could be carried out during the summer weather, but as it is now found that it will have to be done in the winter, the Contractors require an additional 1s per square yard.' During the re-decking, single-line working was employed on the pier. The work was completed by June 1907. The final bill was 'about £12,000', but that sum included some permanent way renewal and incidental work.

The record for 7th January 1908 refers to the 'Portsmouth and Ryde Letter Mail Contract': an increased payment to the Joint Committee, it was revealed, included 'the conveyance of mails in the night mail train worked between Ryde Pier Head and St.John's Road Stations by the Isle of Wight Company, and that the payment of £30 a year hitherto made to the Joint Committee will therefore cease'.

Porter Shepherd was tried at the Winchester Assizes on two charges of stealing jewellery of the total value of £447 from the railway premises at Ryde, and was sentenced in January 1915 to six months' imprisonment with hard labour.

Any pier of course was vulnerable to damage, given the vagaries of weather and at about 1.0pm on 18th March 1918, the motor boat Krom, owned by the obviously unlucky Messrs. Pickfords Ltd, collided with and damaged the eastern side of the pier, displacing one of the columns supporting the girders, bending the bottom flange of one girder and fracturing some bracing. Notice was promptly given that the joint Committee held them responsible. It was a bad winter, for in January about a hundred 9-foot lengths of 3-inch cast-iron water main on Ryde Pier 'burst from frost'.

On 4 April 1922 a report from the Engineers called attention to the heavy cost of maintaining the pier. It was

In this undated picture, passengers disembark from SHANKLIN at Ryde Pier. According to Dendy Marshall's sometimes erratic 'History of the Southern Railway', the vessel was built by Thorneycroft and entered service on the Portsmouth - Southsea - Ryde run in 1924.

Until the SR era, there were only three platform faces at Ryde Pier Head station, the later addition being the platform seen here on the extreme right. The original platform numbering ran from west to east (from right to left in this view), but was subsequently reversed. The platforms labelled 2 and 3 in this picture were, therefore, originally 2 and 1 respectively.

1. Provision of modern and faster boats - 'The two older boats will be improved'.

2. The running of the steamers to and from Stokes Bay during foggy weather, or making arrangements to ensure passengers from the Isle of Wight will reach London before noon - 'The question of running steamers in foggy weather must rest with the Captains'.

3. Better accommodation for the transport of horses between Ryde and Portsmouth - 'This will have consideration'.

4. A steamer to run in connection with the 6.40pm train from Waterloo all year round - 'A connection is made daily in the three summer months and two days a week during the other nine months, and the question of extending this will be considered'.

5. The boats in connection with the express trains to run direct between Portsmouth Harbour and Ryde without calling at Southsea - 'Some boats do this already, but it would not be possible for all to do thus without losing a large amount of revenue'.

6. Steamboats to be berthed bow outwards where time permits, as time is wasted by boats having to turn after passengers are on board - 'The difficulties of navigation at Portsmouth Harbour render this impossible'.

7. Provision of a covered way on Ryde Pier between the Steamer and the Station - 'To carry this out would mean covering in the whole of the pier between the station and the three berthing places, and this, besides being objectionable in fine weather, would interfere with the transfer of heavy luggage'.

The Southern era - and after

At the grouping, the Southern Railway acquired Ryde Pier and, of course, all the other railways on the island. The old pier at Ryde became SR property in 1924, but the new proprietors were

built of wooden piles, and they had been much damaged by 'marine creatures', demanding constant attention and renewal. Reconstruction in ferroconcrete was recommended, at an estimated cost of £50,000, the work being spread over three or four years. The General Managers advised that the station buildings should also be reconstructed at the same time.

In the Minutes, one subject cropped up every single year. It was the Joint Committee's unfaltering approval of a subscription of £5 towards the Town Cup - one of the events of the Royal Yacht Club Regatta at Ryde.

As for the ferry services between Portsmouth and Ryde, on 15 July 1913 representatives of the Isle of Wight Council put a few questions to the general managers of the Joint Committee. The minutes took the form of 'questions and answers', the answers being, on the whole, spectacularly noncommittal:

Esplanade station in December 1966 - just a few weeks before the end of scheduled steam-hauled workings on the Isle of Wight. The line to St John's Road station is in the mid-distance on the left, the 'station' in the centre of this picture being that of the old tramway. One of the Drewry cars is evident - the two vehicles (latterly Nos 7 and 8) were fitted with diesel engines in 1959/60, and remained in action until services ceased in January 1969.

Esplanade station photographed from the Esplanade. This was the west side of the station in December 1966 - the tramway premises are nearer the camera, with the line to St. John's Road behind.

parallel single lines between there and St.John's Road could be worked as a conventional double track during the summer season. That however, had no direct effect on the St.John's Road - Esplanade - Pier Head section, which was always worked as a conventional double-track line.

The face of Isle of Wight motive power changed during the 1920s and 1930s, most of the native locomotives being pensioned off and replaced by ex-LSWR 'O2' 0-4-4Ts and former-LB&SCR 'E1' and 'Terrier' 0-6-0Ts. ('Terriers' had, in fact, been purchased by two of the pre-grouping companies on the Isle of Wight, the Southern transferring three more between 1927 and 1930). It appears that no special restrictions applied to any type of locomotive working on Ryde Pier.

After the inevitable hiatus to the holiday trade during World War II, visitors soon started to return to the Isle of Wight *en masse* and, although some

The less-homely side of the Isle of Wight railways, perhaps. This very much non-picture-postcard view, taken in April 1950, shows the mess accommodation for the CCE's staff at Esplanade station.

faced with the problem of antiquated stock and equipment. New electric stock wasn't the answer, as there were no means of generating additional electricity for more-modern vehicles, and so, in 1927, the SR replaced the electric trams by a pair of Drewry petrol railcars. In 1935, one of the Drewry cars had to be replaced after an accident but, apart from the cars being fitted with diesel engines in 1959/60, they continued operating until the cessation of services in January 1969.

During the 1920s, there was a dramatic upsurge in the holiday traffic to the Isle of Wight, the increase continuing until the outbreak of war in 1939. A large proportion of the visitors arrived at Ryde, and this put a strain on the town's railways. To help cope with the extra traffic, in May 1926 a signalbox was installed at Smallbrook Junction (nearly one mile south of St.John's Road station) so that the

Is there something peculiarly fascinating about a holiday resort out of season? There is to me but, each to his own... This picture was taken in January 1958, possibly in preparation for the reconstruction of the pier which was undertaken later that year. The section behind the railings on the left is that used by the tramway, the railway section being out of view (farther to the left).

tember 1966. The engineering department subsequently took possession of Ryde Pier to carry out maintenance work (principally at the seaward end) and to undertake track alterations at the Pier Head station. While the pier was out of action, services terminated at Esplanade. Due to the lack of run-round at Esplanade station, an engine was attached to the rear of incoming trains at St.Johns Road, the 'rear' engine subsequently taking the train back out to Shanklin, while the 'front' engine ran light from St.John's Road to the shed for servicing.

The alterations at Pier Head station were largely concerned with the electrification of the line in preparation for the arrival of former London Transport electric tube stock, for use on the island's remaining line. The ex-LT stock arrived in dribs and drabs throughout the autumn, and at the end of 1966 all services on the entire Ryde - Shanklin line ceased so that the necessary work could be undertaken for the inauguration of the electrics. Public services - with the electric stock - between Ryde Pier Head and Shanklin recommenced on 20 March 1967.
Contributor's note: Sincere thanks are due to Messrs. Eric Youldon, Bryan Wilson and Chris Hawkins for their assistance during the preparation of the text.

Left : These two (date unknown but pre-1956) pictures were taken in connection with the proposed alterations to the facade of Esplanade station. The buses and coaches, then as now, stood close alongside awaiting the connections, and the white caps of the Southern Vectis crews are highly visible on the right in the view from the road.

Below : Esplanade at an unrecorded date - the 'Southern Railway' notice (on the right), is no guide, for these signs lingered over the island (most notably at Cowes, until closure - see for instance *An Illustrated History of the Isle of Wight Railways, Cowes to Newport,* Irwell Press, 1993).

of the island's more-rural lines and stations saw a significant drop in trade in the 1950s (resulting in some closures), it was estimated that, during July and August, some 50,000 passengers passed through Ryde Pier each Saturday. The pier was partly reconstructed during the winter of 1958/59, single-line working being used until the work had been completed.

By the 1960s, road transport had taken much of the traffic from the two remaining Isle of Wight lines (Ryde - Cowes and Ryde - Ventnor), and in 1964 it was proposed to close then completely. Reason nevertheless prevailed, as the local roads couldn't possibly have accommodated the summer Saturday Ryde - Shanklin traffic. Although the Ryde - Cowes line succumbed to the axe (in February 1966), and the Ventnor line was truncated at Shanklin (in April 1966), the Ryde - Shanklin section remained open. The last regular steam-hauled working to Ryde Pier Head operated on 17 Sep-

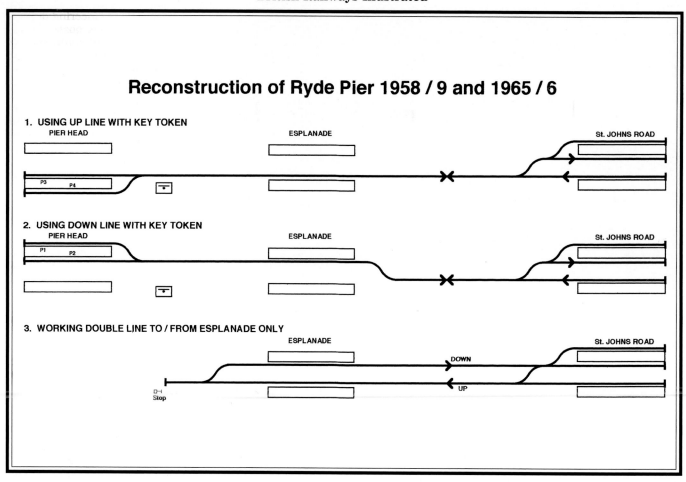

Reconstruction of Ryde Pier 1958 / 9 and 1965 / 6

1. USING UP LINE WITH KEY TOKEN

PIER HEAD   ESPLANADE   St. JOHNS ROAD

P3   P4

2. USING DOWN LINE WITH KEY TOKEN

PIER HEAD   ESPLANADE   St. JOHNS ROAD

P1   P2

3. WORKING DOUBLE LINE TO / FROM ESPLANADE ONLY

ESPLANADE   St. JOHNS ROAD

DOWN

UP

Stop

Below : The remodelled entrance to Esplanade station was photographed in July 1956 - the two sections of the photograph do not quite match, hence the contemporary home-made join. Given the angle of the shadows, expert photographers will be able to determine that the picture was taken just before midday. The scene is charming and summery - though the chalked message announces that the day's cruise is cancelled *due to gale force winds...*

Esplanade station frontage, July 1956.

Trouble at t'Pier. No.22 BRADING, derailed, is passed by No.21 SANDOWN, Saturday 19th June 1965; a fraught day no doubt, for the operating people. Photograph Colin L. Caddy.

SOUTHERN RAILWAY TO THE
ISLE OF WIGHT

Express Services from London (WATERLOO) via Portsmouth and Ryde, only 30 minutes sea crossing.

CHEAP FARES FROM

WATERLOO:	"Monthly"		Tourist.				"Monthly"		Tourist.	
	1st	3rd	1st	3rd			1st	3rd	1st	3rd
Ryde ...	21/9	14/6	25/3	17/3	Cowes ...		25/6	17/0	29/6	20/0
Seaview	22/6	15/3	26/0	18/0	Newport		24/6	16/3	28/3	19/3
Sandown	23/9	15/9	27/3	18/6	Yarmouth		26/9	17/9	32/3	22/0
Shanklin	24/0	16/0	27/6	18/9	Fresh-					
Ventnor	25/3	16/9	29/0	19/9	water		27/0	18/0	31/9	21/6

NOTE.—All above fares are via Portsmouth. Fares via Southampton or Lymington are slightly different. Children under 14 Half Price.

"MONTHLY RETURN" TICKETS at a PENNY-A-MILE are issued from all parts throughout the year, on any day, and by any train. (London Fares shown above.) They are available for return any time within a month from the day of issue.

TOURIST TICKETS are issued any day May to October, by any train, available three months.

Through trains from NORTH, MIDLANDS, WALES, etc., in connection with steamers   Cheap Fares.

When Staying in the Isle of Wight

SEE THE ISLAND with a

7-DAY "ALL-ISLAND" SEASON TICKET
(issued from APRIL 1st—OCTOBER 31st),
covering the 32 Isle of Wight Stations. Price
10/6 1st class: **7/6** 3rd class (Children
under 14 Half-Price).

7-DAY SEASON TICKETS covering all Stations in the Island, also including S.R. Steamers between RYDE and SOUTHSEA PIER HEADS (Clarence and South Parade) and PORTSMOUTH **18/-** 1st class; **15/-** 3rd class rail, 1st class boat.

For further particulars and information apply S.R. Stations & Enquiry Offices.

Above : 27 MERSTONE stands above the unwelcoming waters, 21st July 1965. Photograph M.S. Castledine.

Above : Come winter, the meagre attractions at Esplanade withdrew into themselves, rather as the peeler crabs, used for bait close by, slipped gratefully into their new-found shells. The constant to and fro of the summer gave way to an intermittent activity as islanders went about their business - by this time (1966) a rare enough activity, and Esplanade relied almost wholly on the Portsmouth traffic - principally shopping as far as the islanders were (and are) concerned.

Top left : Inside Esplanade station - hardly a fitting gateway to 'The Eden Isle'.

Left :A fascinating, if unusual viewpoint of Esplanade station frontage, December 1966.

Right : Ryde Pierhead in August 1964 with No.14 about to depart for Ventnor; paddle steamer Ryde is on the right. Photograph Peter Groom.

Left : The Esplanade at Ryde, photographed from the old pier in December 1966.

Above : Esplanade station, looking towards the pier, December 1966. It seems that preparatory work for the impending electrification was already in hand.

Left : Ryde Pier, looking towards the Pier Head, December 1966.

Right : Vans on the Pier, with No.22 BRADING - date would appear to be about 1957. Photograph Hugh Davies.

Above : The archetypal British beach - determined sun bathing at Ryde in the last days of the season, 11th September 1959 - and who could resist this for the BRILL *Summer Special?* Today the water would be declared poisonous, the sand unsafe for bare human feet, deckchairs would be outlawed unless tested and passed under regulation 114 Eurosub-section 73(c) governing 'industrial-type relaxant apparatus'; the Pier would be condemned and the train banned for dangerous fumes and exhaust likely to set fire to bathers' costumes. Sun block would be compulsory and sunbathers ordered to cover up (by uniformed inspectors) after the specified 22.4 minutes, and police would be holding back a 'Stop Cruelty to Donkeys' demo. Photograph Eric Sawford.

Below : Getting those holidaymakers (when did we cease to be 'holiday makers' and become 'tourists'?) down to the boarding houses of Sandown, Shanklin and Ventnor. No.35 FRESHWATER on the Pier, 18th May 1964. Photograph Leslie Sandler.

Above : The Tram, 1st November 1928. Photograph H.C. Casserley.

Below : Back to the Pier Head, and a tired No.26 WHITWELL on 21st July 1965. The name of A.B. MacLeod runs prominently through the story of the Isle of Wight railways. He was in charge of the Loco Carriage and Wagon Department from 1928 and had a hand in many of the Island developments - including that extended O2 bunker. In his *Narrative* is the amusing account of the old lady and the Pier. It was always a 'mass of scurrying people', with some 36,000 people using the trains on a summer Saturday - and that total excluded many who used the tram or walked. The staff at Pier Head had been unable to convince the old lady to leave the train - she had, after all, been assured by the Shanklin stationmaster that *this was the Waterloo train...*

Above : 18 NINGWOOD and 26 WHITWELL together at the Pier Head, with PS SANDOWN in the background, 28th July 1963. Photograph Phil Lynch.

Below : The embarrassed BRADING again, derailed on Saturday 19th June 1965, now with 28 ASHEY to the rescue with the breakdown gang and train. Photograph C.L. Caddy.

Above : 16 VENTNOR at Esplanade,11th September 1959. Photograph Eric Sawford.

Below : MERSTONE comes to a stand at Pier Head, 21st July 1965. That bunker shows to good effect here - MacLeod tells the story of these in his *Narrative;* the Ryde to Ventnor service was experiencing a continual increase in passengers and a further revision in the timetable was made in 1933, "with a view to providing for an increased service for summer Saturdays when the fourth platform at Pier Head would be available". The O2s on this new service, which was to give three trains each way Ryde to Ventnor, one to Sandown and one to Newport and Cowes in each direction every hour from ten in the morning to 6 o'clock teatime, had to last longer in traffic between taking coal, and MacLeod determined upon a doubling in capacity to three tons. A GW-type experiment was abandoned and this version arrived at, fitted first to No.26 WHITWELL. Photograph M.S. Castledine.

Above : MERSTONE takes water at the Pier Head, 13th July 1966. Photograph M.S. Castledine.

Below : Delicious endpiece. No.17 SEAVIEW with replacement nameplates, begins to run round at the Pier Head, very near The End, 13th July 1966. Photograph M.S. Castledine.

FOURUM
Keith Shed

Keith shed, a rural byway, in early BR days, around 1949 - smokebox numberplates yet to appear on ex-Great North 4-4-0s D40 No.62264 and D41 62247. Photograph Neville Stead Collection.

Still fairly early on in BR days, though after May 1951 - the D40 on the left still awaits a smokebox plate - engines from left to right are the aforementioned D40, a Caledonian 3F 0-6-0 (possibly 57591 or 57634) then a B12 4-6-0, a GNoS 4-4-0, two B1s, and 62277 GORDON HIGHLANDER (now preserved). Photograph Neville Stead Collection.

Keith on 11th August 1956. 62267, mournful in the rain, was withdrawn that very month, so is probably already out of use. Keith was a meeting place of the Highland and the Great North of Scotland and each company maintained an engine shed in the little town. Both buildings were pretty much ramshackle by Nationalisation and the HR line engines moved to the GNoS premises soon after. The building - note the new girdering and roof - was reconstructed in 1954. The Caledonian 4-4-0, No.54472, would have worked in on an Inverness - Aberdeen train, to join with an Elgin - Aberdeen train at Cairnie Junction, some miles to the south east of Keith, leaving the CR 4-4-0 to return to Keith light engine. There were further peculiarities in the reverse direction, and for long Aberdeen - Inverness trains, which changed engines at Keith, from GNoS to HR, conducted this otherwise conventional procedure *outside* the station. Photograph P.B. Booth, Neville Stead Collection.

14th June 1960 - a BR Standard, Mogul No.76106, marking the march of the years into the BR period. Other engines are a J36 0-6-0, a Black 5 and CR 0-6-0 No.57591. Stored in the yard, on the road which had housed old 62267, is a K2 Mogul and a couple of LM 2P 4-4-0s, doubtless more or less abandoned. The nearest might be 40604. At this time, Keith was being given K2s on their last legs and the one in the picture might have been 61779 (withdrawn May 1960), 61782 (withdrawn June 1960) or 61792, withdrawn September 1960. Keith shed closed to steam in June 1961. Photograph D. Butterfield, Neville Stead Collection.

Southern Contrast

All our railways exhibited a wild variety of working, a joyous abundance that went beyond contrast and well into the realm of downright contradiction. Or, at least, it can seem so to us now - it was after all, only the natural reflection of busy, prestigious trunk route *versus* pottering byway. We must remember it was not a show designed for steam enthusiasts - though it could seem a bit like it at times... After the Second World War the railways looked forward to serving the Nation in a different way, as an arm of the State, and there was no great political division on the subject - the country was in a corporatist frame of mind after all and whilst the political battle moved to and fro across the field of nationalisation in other industries, the railways were not directly assailed until recent times, unless the roads and their champions be cast in such a role.

This then was the sort of contrast to be found upon the Southern (all the other companies could exhibit differences just as dramatic and compelling) after the War and before BR became established. Above: 21C13 BLUE FUNNEL LINES departing Platform 11 at Waterloo with a special train for Exeter, after its naming ceremony there that day, attended by Blue Funnel Chairman Mr. Lawrence Holt, on 17th April 1945. Engine is in wartime black. Photograph BAJT.
Right: an 0-4-4T, M7 No.109, a world away from the bustle of Waterloo, approaching Medstead (on the LSW Alton-Winchester line) in 1948. The engine got its BR number in May the following year. Photograph E.C. Griffith.

Standard Class 5 leads a B1 4-6-0 near Tulloch with a Fort William - Glasgow train in August 1960. Photograph S.C. Crook.

The Stuff of Legend

Building the West Highland Railway

On the Moor of Rannoch, for instance, where the line will require special attention, there is not a house to be seen for miles... By H. Laird

The West Highland line between Craigendoran and Fort William is indeed the stuff of legend. It crosses some of the most wonderfully bleak landscape anywhere in Britain, but while that might partly explain the route's widespread appeal today, that delight was hardly uppermost in the minds of those who planned and constructed the line.

Much has been written about the West Highland Railway - and justifiably so. It is not, therefore, the intention here to attempt yet another corporate history - the emphasis of this particular offering is on the construction of the line and its civil engineer-

ing features. That said, a brief background history will not go amiss.

As for photographs, any recording the actual construction are, for very good reasons of 'logistics' (not a term,

thankfully, in common currency in the 1890s) akin to hens' teeth. We have solved the problem in a hopefully satisfactorily fashion, I hope the reader will agree, with a selection of latter day

The summit board at Corrour has had different wording from time to time and has suffered badly from the elements. This is how it looked in 1938. Photograph J.L. Stevenson.

Photographing trains on a West Highland viaduct is not to be recommended. The photographer admitted to considerable terror as K2 No.4684 LOCH GARRY approached on the 3.46pm from Glasgow, near Tyndrum in 1938. Never again... Photograph J.L. Stevenson.

steam photos, principally from the glorious (if familiar to some) collection held in the *Rail Archive Stephenson* and from the camera of James Stevenson, emboldened by youth and clinging apprehensively to diverse viaducts, crags and posts.

Lines to the West Coast

Some might consider it odd that a railway across seemingly endless miles of uninhabited land was ever considered at all but, of course, the West Highland was not the only railway to strike out for the west coast of Scotland. Strome Ferry in Ross & Cromarty was reached by the Dingwall & Skye Railway in 1870, the line being extended (by the Highland Railway) to the Kyle of Lochalsh in 1897, and the Callander & Oban Railway (which was worked by the Caledonian) opened throughout to Oban in 1880. A number of other schemes for lines to north west Scotland were promoted, but failed to come to fruition. The attraction of the West Coast was basically threefold - fish from the ports and the islands, sheep from north west Scotland to the southern markets and tourists. Into the mix, to a great extent, also went corporate rivalry.

One of the other major Scottish railway companies - the North British - tried its hand (albeit indirectly) in the early 1880s. It took a close interest in the independently-promoted Glasgow & North Western Railway which proposed a line from Glasgow to Inverness via Fort William and Fort Augustus. That proposal met with considerable opposition, not least of all from the Caledonian Railway, and the scheme eventually failed. For a while, it seemed that the important town of Fort William was not to get a railway, and it also appeared that the North British was not going to penetrate the West Highlands. However, in 1889 the NBR put forth its full corporate weight behind the newly-promoted West Highland Railway. The new scheme incorporated a section of the route which had featured in the abortive Glasgow & North Western scheme, but among the many significant differences between the WHR and the G&NWR were, firstly, a starting point at Craigendoran on the existing NBR Clyde Coast line and, secondly, a detour across Rannoch Moor via Tulloch and Spean Bridge. The West Highland Railway finally obtained its Bill on 12th August 1889.

Among the many stories about the WHR's formative years, one of the best-known is that of the 'expeditionary party' which set out on foot to reconnoitre part of the prospective route across Rannoch Moor. The party of seven included at least one 60 year-old gentleman, and only one of the party had ever previously walked across the moor. This could be a recipe for difficulty, even on a fine summer's

K2 61788 LOCH RANNOCH and Stanier Black 5 No.44970 with a Fort William - Glasgow express near Roy Bridge, 30th March 1959. Photograph Rail Archive Stephenson, original by D.M.C. Hepburne-Scott.

The pair leaving Tulloch on the same train. Photograph Rail Archive Stephenson, original by D.M.C. Hepburne-Scott.

BR Standard 4-6-0 No.73077 with a Glasgow - Fort William train climbing away from Tyndrum on 2nd August 1961. Photograph Rail Archive Stephenson, original by D.M.C. Hepburne-Scott.

day - but this hike was undertaken in January. It proved to be a catalogue of calamities. The party's guide failed to turn up, their pre-arranged overnight resting place was not prepared, they got lost the following day, and throughout all this the weather was wet, windy, and cold. Some members of the party collapsed with exhaustion, but two eventually managed to find a shepherd's cottage and subsequently organised the rescue of their colleagues. The whole episode came perilously close to being a major tragedy and, as if to remind the men how lucky they were, a severe blizzard began very shortly after the last had been rescued.

Construction

The building of this hundred miles of railway through the West Highlands and across Rannoch Moor presented a stiff challenge, as may well be appreciated. The engineers appointed to construct the line were Formans & McCall, a firm which had been formed in 1828, and had been responsible for the engineering of some of Scotland's earliest railways.

The contractors were Lucas & Aird who, although London-based, had a Scottish connection in that one of the partners, John Aird, came from a Highland family. That tenuous Scottish link was not, however, the only reason Lucas & Aird clinched the contract. As explained by John McGregor in his recent book *100 Years of the West Highland Railway*, when Lucas & Aird were awarded the contract they took up a block of shares, which the NBR undertook to purchase when the line was ready. Speculation was certainly in the air.

The contractors came under considerable local pressure to employ Highland labour. However, suitable navvies living in the immediate vicinity were hardly numerous, and those who lived farther afield (or on the Western Isles) were usually too poor to pay their fares to the sites. Consequently, Lucas & Aird offered to pay for the travel of suitable applicants, and soon built up an adequate work force.

John Thomas, in his book *The West Highland Railway*, quotes a report of 30th June 1890 which revealed that, on the Helensburgh and Arrochar section, 34 of the 80 men employed had come on paid passages, as had 33 of the 61 on the Inverarnan section, 42 of the 85 on the Tyndrum section, and 69 of the 74 on the Fort William section. Men working south of Ardlui were paid an average of 15/- per week, those employed north of Ardlui (i.e. on the less-hospitable sections) being paid an average of 21/- per week. It may be that the contractors were well aware of a predilection for strong refreshment among their workers, for part of the wages were paid in foodstuffs. A well-fed navvy might be more useful than a well-oiled one. At its peak, the labour force was some 5,000 strong. However, in July 1891 a dispute arose between the contractors and the railway company, and all but 1,200 men were laid off. The dispute was extremely protracted, and it was the spring of 1892 before construction was once again in full swing.

Completion

Partly because of the hiatus in 1891/92, the line was not completed until the summer of 1894. The line was inspected for the Board of Trade by Major Marindin, who tested the bridges on the southern section in May and made a six day inspection of the whole route in June. His report, dated 4 July, concluded that 'by reason of the incompleteness of the works' the West Highland could not be opened for passenger traffic 'without danger to the public using same'.

A further inspection followed shortly, but the report (dated 18th July) again drew attention to the inadequacy of the work - the problem was that much of the equipment and buildings had simply not been finished. The Board of Trade was used to the odd finishing touches put to booking offices, toilets and so on as the first passengers came through the gates but this was a different situation altogether, and there was even work outstanding with respect to the signalling... Facing safety points at Craigendoran Junction were ordered taken out and, rather more fundamentally, the signal cabins were ordered to be completed *'and to be roofed'(!)* at Glendouglas, Ardlui, Crianlarich, Bridge of Orchy, Gorton (later referred to as Gortan, presumably to avoid confusion with the other 'Gorton' inherited by the LNER at the Grouping), Rannoch, Corrour, Inverlair (renamed Tulloch on 1st January 1895), Roy Bridge, Spean Bridge and Fort William. Point and signal connections were also necessary, and proper diagrams were ordered in the cabins together with electric tablet instruments 'to be fixed and brought into use'. Electric repeaters were to be provided for both distant signals at Upper Helensburgh, Row (spelling officially altered to Rhu on 24th February 1927), Shandon, Glendouglas (often known as Craggan in the early days), Ardlui, Tyndrum, Roy Bridge, Spean Bridge and Banavie Junction (subsequently known as Mallaig Junction), for the up distant signals at Arrochar and Tarbet and Crianlarich, and for down distant signals at Garelochhead, Crianlarich, Rannoch, Corrour and Fort William.

A further indication - if any were needed - of the outstanding works is provided in the following extract which details the demands for alterations in interlocking and signalling:
At **Craigendoran West** - railway outside cabin to be lowered. At **Upper Helensburgh** - provide disc at facing points of siding. At **Row** - clear view of

K1/1 61997 - regular readers will be familiar with the life and times of this loco from *That's Progress* in the April 1995 edition of *British Railways Illustrated*. Fort William, June 1954. Coaches are departmental? Photograph Rail Archive Stephenson, original by E.V. Fry.

*Home signals by lopping trees; remove runaway points on up loop. At **Shandon** - interlock Nos.11 and 6 levers. At **Arrochar & Tarbet** - remove runaway points and fix disc at facing points of siding. At **Crianlarich** - provide second down distant signal. At **Tyndrum** - provide runaway points on down loop. At **Bridge of Orchy** - complete level crossing gate. At **Gortan** - provide runaway points on down loop. At **Rannoch** - interlock Nos.9 and 15 levers; remove runaway points. At **Corrour** - remove runaway points on*

*down loop. At **Inverlair** - provide runaway points on up loop. At **Banavie Junction** - No.9 lever to precede No.4. At **Fort William** - No.23 lever not to follow No.19; interlock Nos.4 & 5 with No.17; clear view of station from the cabin; provide signal frame on platform with levers to slot up Home signals, to work discs in the cabin, and to work points of cross-over road.*

Further buildings at stations and platforms had to be completed, at Crianlarich, Tyndrum, Rannoch, Inverlair and Roy Bridge. The fencing

of the line at Bridge of Orchy, Rannoch, Corrour and several other places in the northern section had to be completed - brick posts and rails were specified in hollows, whilst cross banks and walls running up to the line were to be fenced. 'Hummocks' at the back of fences were to be levelled down where necessary and wing wall fences at many of the bridges had to be made good. The list of requirements is one of the most comprehensive in all the BOT records - just the 'sundries' run out as follows -

The B1s did a fair amount of work between Glasgow and Fort William, though with only moderate success. 61197 is paired with a new K1, No.62030, in September 1949, the pair climbing well at 1 in 59 on the last part of the long slog alongside Loch Treig, from Tulloch to Corrour summit. Photograph J.L. Stevenson.

Winter, cruel and cold - Gorton Crossing in the middle of Rannoch Moor, February 1951. Lying snow and the promise of more made for a truly menacing picture. Needless to say, there were operating difficulties. Photograph J.L. Stevenson Collection.

- Hand rails on many of the underbridges to be fixed.
- Fitting of check rails on the sharp curves and of outside guards on the viaducts and 3-span underbridges to be completed.
- All wooden platforms of underbridges to be covered with gravel as a protection against fire.
- All temporary siding points on the line to be removed except those at 1m 23ch, 80m 59ch, 90m 45ch and 98m, which are to remain in, and for the working of which frames locked by the Train Tablet must be provided.
- All Contractors' coal stages and water tanks to be removed.
- The curves at 7m 60ch, 12m 10ch, 21m and 32m to be adjusted.
- The permanent way on the spur line at Crianlarich, on 2 miles of line north of Auch viaduct, on Corrour up loop and at Auchardill siding to be completed.
- Ballasting at places to be completed and the line to be straightened and lifted at places and fish plate bolts to be made good.
- The line to be slewed away from plat-form on the up loop line at Arrochar & Tarbet, nearer to the platform on the up loop and away from the platform on the down loop at Ardlui, also through the tunnel and along the cemetery retaining wall at Fort William.
- Curve entering station loop at South End of Crianlarich Station to be improved.
- Footbridge at Craigendoran and two other stations to be completed and subways at others paved.
- Padlocks to be fitted to all field gates and the hanging of one set of gates to

Crianlarich, 12th April 1958, and 44787 with 61786, leaving with a Fort William - Glasgow train. Photograph Rail Archive Stephenson, original by D.M.C. Hepburne-Scott.

be altered.
- Deficient rivets in Bridge girders at 92m 44ch and 99m 7ch to be made good.
- Concrete apron at abutment of Bridge at 97m 61ch to be made good.
- A 4-foot cast-iron pipe culvert to be put in near the 52nd mile post.
- Ramp leading to platform at Upper Helensburgh to be covered by roof, and screens on overbridge to be completed.
- Screens to be fixed at Crossconar Bridge and at the County March near Tyndrum.

- The wooden culverts at 62m 6ch, and between 70m 38ch and 71m 79ch (especially one at 71m 53ch) are rather distorted and must be carefully watched.
- The line in places on Rannoch Moor, on the Gaur and Cruach banks and over the Moss at 96m 50ch will require constant attention until it is properly consolidated.
- Signalmen's cottages at the passing places to be finished.
- An undertaking on the usual form as to the working of the line and a certifi-

cate as to the quality of the steel used in the bridges was 'to be furnished'.

There was more - certain speed limits were imposed (more of which anon) whilst at Craigenarden on Loch Lomondside the road alongside the railway was found to be dangerous owing to its position between the railway and a precipitous bank falling into deep water. 'A screen' was proposed but it was regarded as a question for the road authorities whether a wall along the Loch side or a screen along the railway would be the better safe-

The Highlands have ever been a place of contrast and the men who built it would have been familiar with them - visibility hardly beyond your boots one minute, giving way to a clear vista of distant hills the next. Driving, freezing, rain would be followed by glorious sunshine washing gently over the moor and its sudden, cheering warmth on the back of your neck signified the dropping wind and the inevitable onrush of fiendish, biting midges. Low sun in the late afternoon has always been a particular glory of these wild lands and is reflected wonderfully from 44968 and 61774 on an evening Fort William - Glasgow train. Photograph Rail Archive Stephenson, original by W.J. Verden Anderson.

Board of Trade on 3rd August. The report, which was dated 6th August, commented on a number of relatively minor aspects which still needed attention, and also indicated what work was required at the stations. Despite a number of points, the verdict was that the line could be safely opened for passenger traffic, 'subject to the requirements being satisfied, which it was promised should be done'. The requirements were:

'**Upper Helensburgh** - gravelling of platform, and roofing to be completed. **Row** - fitting of WCs, and the waiting rooms on up side to be completed. **Glendouglas** - runaway points on up loop taken out by mistake and to be restored; signal cabin and signalman's house to be completed. **Arrochar & Tarbet** - a little painting and lettering to be done; down distant signal repeater to be provided. **Ardlui** - a little painting and finishing up to be done. **Tyndrum** - ditto. **Bridge of Orchy** - ditto, and roof of signal cabin to be slated. **Gortan** - signal cabin and signalman's house to be completed. **Rannoch** - footbridge, which was broken down by accident with crane, to be rebuilt; some painting and joiner's work etc to be completed. **Corrour** - signal cabin and signalman's house to be completed; down distant signal repeater to be provided. **Inverlair** - permanent buildings to be completed; up distant signal repeater to be provided; at this station temporary buildings with sufficient conveniences have been provided. **Roy Bridge** - A good deal of work, painting, joiner's work and plastering, to be done; cabin to be completed; shelter shed on down platform to be built. **Spean Bridge** - a little painting, lettering and joiners work to be done; shelter shed on down platform to be completed. **Fort William** - temporary buildings with sufficient accommodation have been put up, the permanent buildings to be finished; safety points to be inserted on the line leading from harbour; the view of the up platform from the signal cabin to be cleared'.

The ceremonial opening of the line had been planned for 11th August, but the NBR learned of Major Marindin's decision on Friday 3rd. With thoughts of capitalising on the remaining peak-season traffic, the necessary signalling details were finished in a great hurry on the Sunday night, the contractor's plant cleared and rolling stock brought in on the Monday, and revenue-earning traffic commenced on Tuesday 7th August.

The subject of potential traffic had been addressed in general and, as it transpired, slightly optimistic terms, in *Engineering* magazine on 20th July 1894, a fortnight or so before the line opened:

'It must not be assumed that it (the railway) is only for crofter traffic which, however beneficial to the Highlander, might not be sufficient to insure financial success. At the southern end, the

guard. A second long length of screen, it was thought, might also be necessary in Glenfalloch but it was left to the Perthshire County Council to negotiate with the railway as to its precise arrangements. The railway was also urged ('to lose no time') in building cottages for the station staff and surface men in the sparsely populated portions of the country through which the line passed. The Board of Trade had a warning -'On the Moor of Rannoch, for instance, where the line will require special attention, there is

not a house to be seen for miles and cottages are absolutely necessary for the surface men'.

Regarding the last point, author John McGregor reveals that the problem of housing railwaymen along the route was not finally resolved until 1896, makeshift arrangements having caused much distress and protest in the severe winters of 1894/95 and 1895/96.

Another Look

A re-inspection was carried out for the

The Craigendoran - Arrochar & Tarbert service was usually the province of North British tanks, especially after 1940 when push-pull operation was introduced. On a November afternoon in 1955 C15 No.67474 glides into the West Highland station at Craigendoran - three C15s were equipped for this work, 7460 in 1940 followed by 67474 and 67475, in 1954 and 1950 respectively. Photograph J.L. Stevenson.

Crianlarich on 4th October 1950, and K2 2-6-0 No.61776 crosses the viaduct over Strath Fillan and the Callander and Oban line, with a Fort William - Glasgow Civil Engineer's special - comprised of an eight wheel bogie saloon. Photograph C.C. Herbert.

means of conveyance, and even General Wade's roads were too far distant'. From the first, a telephone system was put in over the course of the work, 'so that at all points immediate and constant communication was possible between the head office and the staff of contractors' engineers, and thus the work progressed with the minimum of inconvenience'.

How to get the plant and material to the site of the work, over such terrain? To overcome this problem, the contractors devised a system of 'depots' at the most convenient points, and 'telescoped' the sections of line from each of these. *Engineering* reveals that the first depot was at Craigendoran, where the new line began, at a junction with the North British. Craigendoran was on the estuary of the Clyde, so *'sea carriage was also available. The next point was at the head of Loch Long; then on the shore of Loch Lomond; next at Crianlarich, where the line crosses the Callander & Oban Railway, to which a connection was made by a short service railway; and, lastly, at Fort William, the terminus, where all plant and material were conveniently delivered by sea'.*

With this system of working, the line was never beyond some ten miles of so of the 'starting-points', apart from the section wherein lay Rannoch Moor - it remained thirty miles from the depot, and the work across the Moor was of consequence 'much later in being undertaken than at other points'.

As could be expected from the nature of the country crossed by the railway, there was a proliferation of bridges. These comprised nineteen structures with three or more spans, 102 with one or two spans, and 227 cattle creeps or stream or accommodation bridges. There were also fifty over-bridges. In a six mile stretch near Loch Treig alone, there were about 100 outlets for 'scour' brought down from the mountains. The superstructures of most of the major bridges were built of steel, the total weight used in construction being some 4,000 tons; they were built on behalf of the contractors by Alexander Finlay & Co of Motherwell. It was estimated that the cost of the steel was around £16 per ton, transportation to the sites adding an average of £2 per ton.

The diverse nature of the local conditions meant that various methods had to be employed for the different structures. One of the largest on the entire line was Glen Falloch Viaduct, which carried the railway over the deepest gulley on the route - Dubh Eas, three miles north of Ardlui and more than thirty miles from Craigendoran. The method of constructing it was described in the 3rd August 1894 issue of *Engineering: 'There are seven spans, six of which are at 51ft 6in centres, or 46ft clear, while the centre span is at 118ft centres. The stream is not of great volume; but like most mountain burns or becks, it attains great volume dur-*

railway places within an hour or an hour and a half's journey of Glasgow, sites on the slopes of the Gareloch, Loch Long, and Loch Lomond, for the residences of Glasgow merchants, and these, alike for situation and prospect, are not to be excelled. Only the absence of convenient means of communication has militated against the extensive use of those districts hitherto, and it is anticipated that there will now be a movement to those western hills, with their bracing atmosphere. Again, the line runs close by many lochs and streams where trout and salmon disport themselves. The railway, indeed, is entitled to be ranked as a tourist line, for the line opens up some charming scenery, for the most part strongly typical of the "land of the mountain and the flood" '.

Despite the optimism exhibited in *Engineering* for the line's prosperity,

there had initially been a degree of uncertainty surrounding the volume of traffic the railway would attract. Consequently, the general guideline issued by the West Highland Railway had been that construction should be as inexpensive as possible. Nevertheless, the final bill worked out at over £1,000,000 - around £10,000 per mile.

How it Had Been Done

Completion of the line was rightly regarded as a magnificent achievement. Various journals of the day devoted considerable space to the new railway, though perhaps the most thorough reports are those contained in five different issues of *Engineering*. The issue for 20th July 1894 pointed out that conditions had been, to say the least, difficult, across ground which for many long miles was 'far removed from

Two Black 5 4-6-0s, Nos.44968 and 44967, leave Tulloch with a Fort William - Glasgow train, 30th September 1959. Photograph Rail Archive Stephenson, original by D.M.C. Hepburne-Scott.

ing floods. The slopes are of rock, with a very thin covering, so that there was no difficulty experienced in forming the foundations for the piers.

'The piers are of concrete, which was mixed on wooden platforms alongside, and deposited within shuttering and carefully levelled off with shovels. The concrete was laid in layers of 9in, and allowed to set before the next layer was put in position.

'When the piers for the centre span had been raised to a little over the level of the banks, a trussed service bridge was erected. One complete truss was pushed forward with the other truss as a back balance till the opposite pier was reached. The remaining truss was then taken over the one secured in position, and launched into place, after which the intermediate connections were fixed and adjusted, and the flooring put on. The operation required great care and skill, but was carried through very successfully.

'The temporary bridge was used for the transport of concrete and all materials required not only for works immediately to the north of the bridge, but also for the subsequent erection in position of the centre span of the viaduct. The bridge was preferred to staging which, owing to the height and to floods, would have been difficult and costly of construction. It is said to be the longest service span yet used in Scotland.

The work of this took about three months; *Engineering* records that some 400 tons of steel were used, an undertaking which in a remote district such as this, *Engineering* described,

A couple of BR Standard 5MTs, Nos.73077 and 73078, spent most of their lives at Eastfield and commonly worked to Fort William. 73077 pilots B1 No.61140 (with self weighing tender) across the Fillan viaduct at Crianlarich on 8th August 1959 while the Callander and Oban line, now abandoned, passes beneath. Photograph Hamish Stevenson.

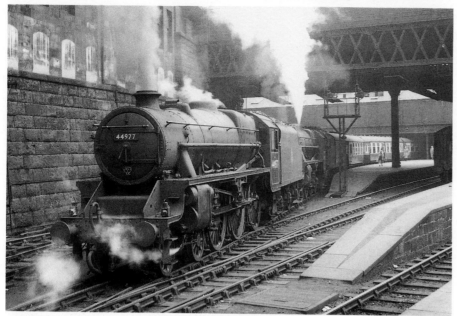

By 1956 LM Class 5s had taken over much of the working and after a shaky start proved very competent. Double heading remained common on the West Highland line in the years of their working, due both to heavy loadings and the frequent unbalance of power. Until Queen Street station was reconstructed the afternoon journey to Fort William usually started from the gloomy east side platform (now mercifully eliminated) - 44977 and 44707 are ready to leave Queen Street on the 3.46pm to Fort William and Mallaig in April 1956. With a banker in the rear the 1 in 41 climb to Cowlairs presented no problem. Photograph J.L. Stevenson.

in curiously understated terms, as 'satisfactory'. The cost of the steel work, excluding transport over the six miles from the pier at Loch Lomond, was about £7,000. The completion of Glen Falloch Viaduct was the key to running ballast trains through to Rannoch Moor - which became critical in the spring of 1894.

Another important structure was Auchtertyre Viaduct in Strath Fillan, about ten miles to the north of Glen Falloch Viaduct. Auchtertyre Viaduct, which carried the railway 112ft above a stream, had five lattice girder spans - four of 50ft span and one of 101ft - on a curve of 12ch radius. It was supported by ashlar ('square hewn masonry') piers. Although the girder work for Auchtertyre Viaduct was very similar to that of Glen Falloch, the former was constructed without the need for a service bridge. The girders for its centre span were built away from the bridge, and run out on bogies on a temporary staging which had been built up from the bottom of the glen, then lowered into position. A similar method was used during the construction of a three-span bridge over a stream at Garelochhead.

At Horseshoe Curve the line traversed a pair of viaducts, one of nine spans and the other of five. The construction of these two was far from easy, but the task had been considered preferable to rerouting the railway in a direct line between the slopes of Ben Odhar and Ben Doran, which would have necessitated a massive and extremely costly single viaduct.

The building of the shorter of the two Horseshoe Viaducts was not helped by the structure being on a curve of 15ch radius, and although the girders were

'launched' into position as at Glen Falloch and Auchtertyre, the method had, of necessity, to be different. For this 'launching' the girders were fixed together end to end, 'having tapered hardwood between so as to take the curves'.... *'The launching arrangement was by sets of trolley wheels running in small frames and acting as loose rollers, rails being secured to the bottom flange of the girders to run on the top of the trolleys. Tackle was supplied to drag the spans forward. The spans being secured at the ends to form a continuous girder as stated, they could be launched right out and counterbalanced safely until the next pier was reached. With substantial and careful arrangements a few hours sufficed for the launching operations of each span.*

This method of operation was not costly, the viaduct of five spans, which weighed around 200 tons, costing for erection and riveting 60s/- a ton'.

The construction of the nine-span Rannoch Viaduct presented different problems. Whilst it would have been preferable to fill in the bog which the railway had to cross, the vast volume of material necessary to fill the 15ft-deep bog and then build a 50ft-high embankment above, made the construction of a viaduct a more practical alternative. The area of the foundation for each pier was timbered, the mossy ground subsequently being excavated down to the level of the boulder clay. The foundations were made of concrete (four parts sand to one of cement - as with most of the works on the entire railway) the concrete being carried up to surface level. The piers were then constructed, the material being granite which had come from Cruach Rock cutting, less than a mile to the north. In common with Glen Falloch Viaduct, that at Rannoch also carried a footway.

The largest arched structure on the line was Craigenarden Viaduct, on the banks of Loch Lomond. Its piers were built of bluish whinstone, the arches being turned in concrete, such a design being preferred to a girder structure out of deference to the beauty of the local landscape. As a finishing touch, the parapets of the viaduct were castellated - a common feature in Scotland where powerful local Lairds often had a considerable say in the cosmetic appearances of civil engineering works on their lands. The viaduct had eight spans, each of 36ft, the rise of each arch being 13ft. The original survey for the route, incidentally, took the line along the shore of Loch Lomond - i.e. with no need for the viaduct - but an eventual revision of the route necessitated its construction.

At the smaller end of the scale were the numerous creeps and overbridges for sheep and cattle. Some were built of stone, others of girders or timber,

Heading the 9.31am Fort William to Glasgow 73077 and 44787, having traversed the Horseshoe and passed the County of March summit, are descending to Strathfillan. They are about to enter Tyndrum (Upper) station, April 1961. Photograph J.L. Stevenson.

the comparative costs being listed as:
Wooden bridges, 6ft wide: £160
Lattice girder cattle bridges, 24ft clear span: £200
Plate girder cattle bridge, 24ft clear span: £230
6ft cattle creep: £80
4ft sheep creep: £70

One of the less conspicuous, but nevertheless interesting, features of the line's construction was the method of crossing the mossy bog of Rannoch Moor. *Engineering* again, 20th July 1894: *'The most important step in treating the moss is the arrangement of drainage. The moss varies very much in depth, and the construction had, therefore, to be varied. Turf was cut outside the line of the railway, and all inequalities in the formation level were made up, every effort being put forth to preserve and strengthen the natural surface below formation. Afterwards brushwood was laid down, and this was again covered with moss turf. The depth of brushwood was regulated by the more or less springy nature of the ground. Generally, the brushwood and turf was covered with a layer of mountain till, unless where the line had to be embanked, and upon this formation the ordinary railway sleepers were laid as close together in most cases as was convenient for the packing of the ballast. Meanwhile deep ditches were cut longitudinally on each side of the rails, the distance from the centre of the line being 40ft, while at every 30ft cross drains were cut from the line to the longitudinal drain'.*

The stations

The line was (and still is of course) single. Only a couple of miles separated each station on the first ten miles of route, past Helensburgh and along the Garelochside, 'whither' *Engineering*

observed, 'there is likely to be a migration of Glasgow merchants'. As the line made its way further north into more sparsely populated country, distances between stations increased, to six-ten miles (apart from Rannoch - Inverlair, over 17 miles, the station at Corrour not opening until later). Most stations had island platforms, the double lines making for passing places, while the 'side platform' stations at Row (Rhu), Inverlair (Tulloch), Roy Bridge and Spean Bridge also had passing lines. Where stations were further apart than seven miles or so, intermediate passing loops were provided - at Glen Douglas, Gortan and, initially Corrour. The greatest distance of single line without a passing-place was nine and a half miles

The eleven island platform stations were basically similar to each other, although in the case of platforms built on gradients, the walling was usually of timber, with old sleepers serving for foundations. Ardlui station, at the head of Loch Lomond, was the 'standard' example, described in *Engineering*: *'The length of the platform is 528ft, and the width at centre 35ft, tapering towards the ends. The height from rail level is 3ft, and the distance from the edge of the cope to the outside of the rail is 2ft 2in.*

'The house buildings are in the centre of the platform, with concrete foundations and a granite base course. The buildings are somewhat after the Swiss style, are extremely picturesque, and in keeping with the magnificent scenery with which they are surrounded. The first courses of the walls are of fine brick in cement mortar, while the upper part is of concrete faced with shingles, all got from Switzerland.

'At each end of the buildings there are 5ft screens on each side. The height of

the walls is 9ft 6in, but the roof projects to form a veranda all round, 6ft in width'.

The Fort

At the Fort William end of the line, the railway entered the town from the east and passed along the foreshore to the steam boat pier, close to the passenger station. In preparation for the line, extensive work had to be carried out in banking up the foreshore for a length of some 2,400ft, the resultant wall being up to 12ft high. Whereas the passenger station was at the west end of the embankment, the goods station, engine shed and turntable were at the east end.

Prior to the construction of the railway, various residents of Fort William had raised a number of objections to the proposed route along the shore. The final decision to site the passenger station at the west end of the town was not, in fact, made until late 1893 and, even then, there was still a strong lobby for the siting of the station at the old fort - as had originally been intended.

The differences had (in theory, at least) been settled prior to the West Highland's formal incorporation, the revised arrangements having been drafted for inclusion in the Act of Parliament: *'The Company...shall make the whole surface of the embankment of a uniform height and shall pave the same or otherwise form it to the reasonable satisfaction of the Commissioners (of the Police Burgh of Fort William), and keep the embankment in a proper state of repair in all time coming, and shall sink the rails so that their upper surface shall be on a level with the surface of the Railway and shall have a space of at least fifteen feet between the nearest or Southernmost*

Operation of the West Highland was designed around its regular passing places, as the text relates. This is the system at work - Ardlui in September 1958. Photograph Hugh Davies.

The North British D34 Glens for long gave valuable service on the West Highland. As a final tribute No.62496 GLEN LOY and 62471 GLEN FALLOCH worked the 5.45am from Glasgow to Fort William on 8th and 9th May 1959. The pair are coasting down over the second of the Horseshoe viaducts, getting their breaths back in readiness for the final climb north from Bridge of Orchy. Photograph J.L. Stevenson.

rail and the north or north western boundary wall of or surrounding any of the houses of Fortwilliam (sic), situated between the commencement of said Railway and the termination thereof at (said) public pier and shall make the width of the said Railway extend to a distance of at least eight feet seaward along its whole course beyond the outmost rail and shall complete the surface of the embankment with a substantial fence of an ornamental character and of such height effectually to protect the roadway thus formed; and the Company shall form two suitable boatslips at convenient places and shall also form a sufficient number of culverts of suitable dimensions through the embankments of the Railways to meet the sanitary requirements of the Burgh...The surface of the Railway between the rails and on both sides thereof shall be maintained by the Commissioners and shall be available by the public to be used as a Railway suitable for the use of carts and other vehicles, but such public use to be exercised only to such an extent as shall not interfere in any way with the full use of the rails by the (WHR) Company'.

The townspeople were determined that a 28ft width for the railway and paths etc (as had originally been stipulated) should be maintained.

However, when the WHR's bill had been passed, the good folk of Fort William noticed that the above clause had been omitted. In its place was: '...the company shall make and permanently maintain at their own expense for the free use of the public such footways and carriageways over, under, or across the Railway as the Board of Trade may direct or approve, and shall also construct and maintain at their own expense for the free use of the public on the seaward side of the embankment of the same Railway such

boatslips as the Board of Trade may direct or approve'.

While the railway was under construction at Fort William, the solicitor for the town's police commissioners, Donald McPhee, wrote to the Board of Trade pointing out that the WHR appeared to be making the most of the flexibility offered by the 'revised' clause:

'...a considerable part of the work on the Railway has been satisfactorily done, but they (the Police Commissioners) regret to be obliged to call the attention of the Board of Trade to the erection of the Railway Station at Fortwilliam (sic) on ground which is necessary for preserving the width of 28 feet for the carriage-, rail- and footways...

'In proceeding with the erection of the Station as they are doing and also in erecting a brick signal cabin at the east-

ern end of the Railway, the Railway Company are violating not only the express terms of the adjusted clause...which was inserted for the protection of the Commissioners of Fortwilliam.

'If the Railway with the buildings referred to will be officially approved of and passed by Board of Trade it will be most regrettable. Besides, it is submitted that a roadway of varying widths from 28 to about 12 feet will be a source of danger. This deviation from their original plans is not caused by any engineering necessity but simply on account of the refusal of the proprietor of the Chevalier Hotel at Fortwilliam - a property standing immediately to the south of the station building - to sell the Hotel for less than £7,000 or £8,000.

'Should the Board of Trade hold that the buildings have proceeded too far and that the Company have expended too much money in their erection to be asked to pull them down, then the Railway Company could, with concurrence of the Board of Trade as proprietors of the foreshore, at much less expense widen their embankment northwards and seawards along the entire length of the Station and platforms, to give the 28 feet width arranged for'.

The railway company, possibly mindful of the £300,000-worth of Government aid which was thought to be available for the proposed extension to Mallaig, tugged its corporate forelock and subsequently complied with local wishes.

Early improvements

From the outset the West Highland Railway was leased to and worked by the North British Railway. One almost-perpetual battle between the NBR and the Board of Trade involved the speed limits imposed, Major Marindin having noted in his report of 18th July 1894 that owing to the sharp curves

The onset of the diesels, with Type 2s predominating, took much of the magic out of the line, especially when D6100 or one of its infamous sisters was turned out. Eventually Type 3s - Class 37s - took over the work with much more satisfying results. On a bitterly cold morning in November 1982 No.37085 tops the summit and runs into Corrour station on the 07.00 from Mallaig. Mercifully the steam heating was working well. Photograph J.L. Stevenson.

Fort William shed, with Mogul 61784 on the turntable. Three LOCH nameplates are visible beyond... Photograph Rail Archive Stephenson, original by T.G. Hepburn.

and steep gradients, the speed at many places had to be restricted. He records his pleasure, indeed, at learning of additional time being allowed in the timetable for the trains between Craigendoran and Fort William so that the *average* speed need not be greater than 25 miles an hour. Over certain sections, moreover, he had imposed a *maximum* speed of 20 miles an hour, though several were soon raised by 5mph. Improvements were subsequently made (completed in 1901) to certain sections of the line in the hope of having some of the restrictions eased. The work consisted mainly of easing the curves, and of the addition, throughout the whole length of about 100 miles, of two sleepers per rail length of 24 feet. At the time of the opening of the line, there had been eight, whereas there were now ten sleepers per rail length. The ballasting was also put into a far better condition. The work left the line, the Board of Trade was assured, with no curves of radii less than 12 chains, (formerly 6-10 chains were not infrequent) but whilst the curves were very largely eased, there remained numerous points where reverse curves met without any intervening length of straight road.

Major Pringle of the Board of Trade recommended that the restrictions on four sections of line (a total of only just over ten miles) be raised by 5mph, his report having included the astute observation that: *'The Company have printed the former speed restrictions in*

their Appendix to the Working Time Tables. I do not, however, think that the restrictions are so likely to be observed, when contained in the Appendix in the form of a regulation, as they would be if speed boards were erected at the points noted. The Company concurred in this opinion and agreed to erect speed boards...'

Moreover... *'The Company appear to have lost sight of their undertaking regarding the average speed of trains over the West Highland Railway, for their timetables for July show one train timed to run at an average speed of nearly thirty-two miles an hour, instead of twenty-seven miles* (as was stipulated). Nevertheless, Major Pringle recommended that the average speed for the line be officially raised to 32mph, and after further improvements a 34mph average was authorised in 1905.

It appears that the NBR occasionally took the opportunity of informally sounding out Major Pringle as to what speeds the BoT might accept between Craigendoran and Fort William. Pringle indeed (or a deputy) was a regular visitor to Fort William, as the subsidy for the Mallaig extension was subject to an annual inspection of the line.

When looking at the engineering expertise which went into the building of the West Highland line, it would be wholly unjust to consider only the financial or technical aspects. The working conditions for the men must have been atrocious, made more wearisome by isolation and loneliness, and more

perilous by some of the most capricious weather the British Isles have to offer.

As for the West Highland Railway itself, the inevitable formal absorption by the North British took place in 1908. By then, the West Highland route included the short branch to Banavie (on the bank of the Caledonian Canal to the north of Fort William) which had opened on 1st June 1895, and the extension from Fort William to Mallaig, opened on 1st April 1901. The Mallaig extension, in particular, is a fascinating subject in its own right, not least of all for the famous Glenfinnan Viaduct which was built by 'Concrete Bob' McAlpine. But that's another story...

Contributor's note: Sincere thanks are due to John McGregor of the North British Railway Study Group who, not only offered a wealth of advice during the preparation of this article, but also made available material from his own researches. Many thanks also to Messrs. Marshall Shaw and Brian MacDonald of the NBR Study Group for their invaluable assistance. A special thanks to James Stevenson for photographs and captions.

It is hoped that satisfactory acknowledgements have been made, where appropriate, in the text. Uncredited material, such as Board of Trade reports and extracts from official correspondence, was secured at the Public Record Office, Kew.

DIESEL DAWN Flight of Fancy

As G. Freeman Allen (perceptively, as usual) once wrote, dirt is the sworn enemy of the diesel. It was unfortunate that many BR installations designed to house and maintain the new traction neglected this maxim. Given money, and with engineers let loose to develop new and novel procedures and structures - light and airy was the look, and concrete and glass the materials - it did not have to be so. The Eastern Region based its buildings and practices on a commitment to the operation of heavy diesel electric locomotives, and arrived at a sort of three-tier arrangement - main works, a few big maintenance centres and servicing points at main terminals, far flung outposts and so on. Endearing carry-overs from steam were apparent - like the covered inspection pit (see the wartime 'illuminated pits' discussed at length in **BRILL**) put up at the new Ipswich diesel depot, right, shown in 1961.

At some main depots servicing sheds were provided alongside, or at least in near proximity, to the maintenance depot. Below is the service shed at Tinsley, with D5845 taking fuel in September 1965.

Right top is Stratford 'C' shed, newly open (on the site of the old Jubilee steam building) in August 1960. This formed one end of the depot; 'B' shed was a mirror image at the far end, the two buildings being designed around central stores, offices and workshops sited in between, on an established American model.

Right bottom. An extraordinary building, the service shed at Ripple Lane, new in April 1960. The diesel depots

put up by BR in the late 1950s - early 1960s were a mixed bunch but the emphasis on good design fell away as the money began to run out. But the best of them, like this early clutch of Eastern Region examples, were flights of fancy indeed. Their appearance was largely unremarked, their operating lives unsung and their demise, sadly, unlamented.

On 26th May 1956, 2-4-2T No.50650 rumbles out of the Higham branch carriage sidings, to await departure for Rushden and Higham Ferrers. During her short stay at 15A she rarely worked the similar local service to Northampton and her ex-L&Y stablemate, Bedford's 50646, did very little work at all, spending most of its time in store. Photograph K.C.H. Fairey.

STEAM at WELLINGBOROUGH

A Personal View of 15A by Ken Fairey

It seems only yesterday but over thirty years have passed since the throb of diesel power first made its presence felt at Wellingborough (of course I discount the diesel shunters and the likes of 10000 and 10001). Johnson 0-4-4Ts on the Higham Ferrers and Northampton branches had been replaced in their turn by a variety of tanks, including a Fowler 2-6-2T, an ex-L&Y 2-4-2T, Ivatt 2-6-2Ts and the later Standard BR version. 84007 worked the final Higham Ferrers trains on 13th June 1959. I well remember an unofficial footplate trip with my late father, Driver W.T. Fairey on 50650. She really was an ungainly beast and what a

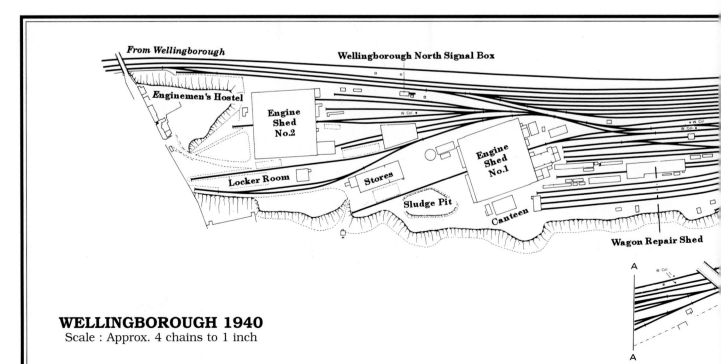

WELLINGBOROUGH 1940
Scale : Approx. 4 chains to 1 inch

During a visit on 29th April 1962, the Mechanical Foreman was insistent that I should take pictures of his new crane. I agreed provided he would arrange for the jib to be lifted and I think the final result was much improved. Photograph K.C.H. Fairey.

rough ride it was up the short branch to Higham Ferrers and back!

Johnson and Fowler 2F, 3F and 4F 0-6-0s were still about on lighter duties and Stanier 8F 2-8-0s had long reigned supreme on the frequent and heavy coal trains to London, until ousted by the BR Standard 9F 2-10-0s. By the late 1950s cleaning was virtually a thing of the past, in fact the only time locomotives were really spick and span was when they returned after shopping at Derby, Crewe or Horwich.

Shunting was a regular part of Wellingborough railway activities. There had always been a stud of 0-6-0 tanks hard at work and well after the 350hp diesels arrived in 1954 there were still eight or nine 'Jocko' 0-6-0Ts allocated to 15A. Endless remarshalling of trains took place, round the clock, and when the wind was in the right direction one could hear the bumpings and bangings of rough shunts late into the night. Duties involved included the quaintly named Tipperary Sidings, the Down Yard, the Old Yard, Neilson's and Henlow sidings and the Station Goods Yard which also incorporated the trip working down to the ex-LNW London Road station (of which more later). Just

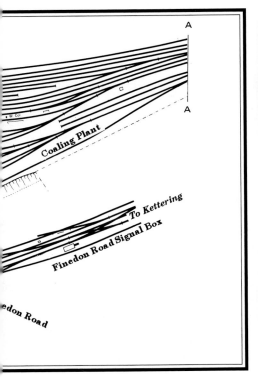

In late 1955, 4F 0-6-0 No.44575 stands in Platform 5 waiting to work up to Higham Ferrers. The engine came new to Wellingborough when I was a lad and as far as I can recollect never wandered far from home. 44575 was a regular performer on the late evening all-stations from Leicester to Wellingborough. Photograph K.C.H. Fairey.

4F No.44574 on 30th June 1960, waiting to leave shed for the Higham parcels trip. It was in that rare condition - clean, after a shopping at Derby works. There is something else out of the ordinary - the smokebox plate and 15A plate have not been painted white, contrary to usual practice. Photograph K.C.H. Fairey.

before World War II we had two ex-G&SWR 0-6-2Ts, 16913 and 16920, for shunting but they were usually reserved for the heavier duties in Henlow sidings. Fortunately one old Wellingborough 'Jocko', 47279, is preserved and working on the Keighley and Worth Valley Railway.

Of course there were several through workings which didn't stop to remarshal at Wellingborough. For many years Fowler 2-6-0 Crabs were the mainstay of the Burton on Trent beer trains up to London and a variety of locomotives worked the down milk empties from Cricklewood which, incidentally, often carried (oddly) a sleeping car. I have even seen a 2-10-0 on this duty. Local passenger jobs on the main line were few and far between from Wellingborough though for many years 40353 was a regular on the

47257 on 6th April 1962, outside the repair shop. Midland Railway practice was to place the repair shop (entered from separate, short turntables, serving each road) immediately at the rear of the 'square roundhouse' building. This shop at Wellingborough was remote from either roundhouse and was so positioned in consideration of the eventual construction (plans were drawn up and even approved) of a third roundhouse. This was never accomplished - see the accompanying diagram. Photograph K.C.H. Fairey.

8F No.48119 heads a freight from the north, bound for nearby Neilson's Sidings, on 24th August 1963. Note the war-time sidings on the right, leading to Finedon Quarry. Once again the scene has completely changed, for there are now only three tracks at this point and roughly where the brake van stands the newly-named Harrowden Junction is located - from this spot just two tracks are enough to handle the present day traffic, until Kettering Junction is reached. Photograph K.C.H. Fairey.

Crab 2-6-0 No.42818 hurries by No.2 shed on one of the up beer trains from Burton-on-Trent. The few Crabs with Reidinger gear were all allocated to Burton and were regular performers on this working. Tipperary Sidings can be seen on the far left together with the large Corn Store with the sidings reception road leading off from the Down Main line. This loop is retained to the present day and often a Class 60 on aggregate empties is held at this point to permit the passage of a down HST. Photograph K.C.H. Fairey.

7.02am local to Leicester interspersed with the occasional 4F 0-6-0. The afternoon 4.58 down local often produced a Class 5 4-6-0. In later years a Nuneaton 'Patriot' often worked in on the early evening local from Northampton depositing its coaches in the (long since lifted) bay platform, going to shed to turn before working back to Northampton later on.

The Midland main line wasn't the first railway at Wellingborough, for the Northampton - Peterborough branch of the London & Birmingham Railway dated from 1845. The loop connecting London Road to Midland Road station came much later. My earliest memories are of ex-LNW Precursors and 2-

On 31st May 1957 45156, one of the named former Scottish Black 5s, waits in the station carriage sidings before taking out the down 4.58pm local from Wellingborough. The fencing is worth a note - of typical Midland style, it flanks the footpath leading from the station to Finedon Road. Photograph K.C.H. Fairey.

4-2Ts but by the late 1950s and early 'sixties most workings were in the hands of Fowler 0-6-0s, 2-6-4Ts or Black 5s. The Northampton - Peterborough workings changed considerably with the arrival of ex-GER Claud 4-4-0s or B1 4-6-0s at Peterborough (Spital Bridge) ex-Midland shed. The working from Peterborough to Northampton, reaching London Road station before 5pm, often produced an Aston Stanier 2-6-0, no doubt a means of returning locomotives to Birmingham after travelling over the Rugby - Peterborough section. The Stanier Moguls were infrequent visitors to the Midland line although on occasion they would turn up on freights from Nuneaton.

A 2P 4-4-0, No.40439, leads 4-6-0 No.45589 GWALIOR (each obviously enjoying a very good head of steam) on an afternoon St. Pancras - Manchester express. The 84000 tank is waiting in the sidings to take out the 3.52pm to Higham Ferrers. Photograph K.C.H. Fairey.

70004 WILLIAM SHAKESPEARE with the 4.25pm St.Pancras - Manchester express on 24th July 1958, overtaking 92160 on a train of empties from London. The Pacifics did well on the Manchester jobs, giving very little trouble. Photograph K.C.H. Fairey.

For many years after the reign of the 2P 4-4-0s and the Compounds, Stanier Class 5 4-6-0s and especially Jubilees, monopolised the express passenger workings through Wellingborough. When special limits were imposed on the train loadings, smaller locomotives were used as pilots and often the shrill whistle of a 2P 4-4-0 or Compound gave a warning as a non-stop express raced pell mell through the station. Nevertheless I have heard several times on good authority that the 4-4-0s, far from playing their part in the hauling, were often pushed! The Jubilees' reign was only broken in the mid-fifties when some Royal Scots became surplus from the West Coast main line and were drafted to the Midland Division. Later still Britannias were allocated to Trafford Park and they made a fine sight (and an even better sound with their chime whistles!) on the Manchester expresses - at the time the Peak

70015 APOLLO on the up Palatine from Manchester, 24th July 1958. In my mind's ear I can still hear those melodious chime whistles, so different from the mournful warning tones emitted from the present-day HSTs. 43624 waits at the Up Slow line signals preparing to pick up the van behind in order to make up the Parcels Trip to Higham Ferrers and back. If not the very last, it certainly came near the end of a long line of 3Fs allocated to Wellingborough. Standing prominent on the bank beside Mill Road bridge is the enginemen's lodging house - so little rest from the sound of wagons and trains in the few hours of sleep! Photograph K.C.H. Fairey.

Inordinate power for the down Palatine on 14th July 1958. BR Class 5 No.73136 and Britannia 70017 ARROW make a spirited start from the station on their way to Manchester. At this time of the morning there is quite a deal of activity - an 84000 2-6-2T waits on the left to leave for Higham and an unseen Standard 5 shunts stock in the Carriage Sidings. Picture taken from Mill Road bridge. Photograph K.C.H. Fairey.and the pre-heating boiler, slung under the conventional one. Photograph K.C.H. Fairey.

District line through Rowsley was still open.

With the depot an 'A' shed, heavy repairs for the whole '15' district, covering Kettering, Leicester and Bedford, were also carried out at Wellingborough - though Leicester af-ter its reconstruction did its own re-pair work. The wheeldrop building also housed the large breakdown crane to-gether with tool vans which were often adequate for minor mishaps without using the large crane. Roundhouse No.2 was used for the heavy repairs and this is the shed still standing though it now serves as a storage building for a large nationally known dried fruit company. Recently, *For Sale* signs have appeared. There is still rail access but little if any use is made of this facility. Wellingborough shed was

2-10-0s Nos.92094 and 92153 making a fine sight on a test train on 15th June 1958. These workings, involving fully fitted coal wagons, foreshadowed a speeding up of freight trains. The reception road entrance to Tipperary Sidings is just by the tender of the second 2-10-0. Photograph K.C.H. Fairey.

5th May 1960, and 8F No.48007 beside the coaler, which stood at the top end of the shed yard. These simple elevators, raising the coal from a pit into which the coal had been 'tippled' (dropped) from adjacent wagons, had their origins in the last days of the LNWR. Before the mechanisation programme which gave us all the familiar, massive concrete coaling plants, with bunkers holding hundreds of tons, got under way, the LMS arranged for one or two installations on a fairly random basis, as and when a particular need arose, and could not be ignored any longer. By this almost accidental way of things Wellingborough acquired this relatively flimsy, inconsequential plant, rather than the concrete tower which characterised so many of its contemporaries. Photograph K.C.H. Fairey.

also used as a staging post for locos travelling to and from London before or after works attention at Derby. Much the same practice was found with the High Peak ex-North London 0-6-0 tanks (as well as other Midland Division types) making their way to Bow Works but strangely enough, I never recall them dropping in on their way northwards.

The Beyer Garratts (so long a feature of the iron ore workings to the north east) disappeared for withdrawal in the late 1950s much to the relief of local firemen who had sweated away in their enclosed cabs. These trains made use of the loop line from the ex-LNW (and earlier L&B) London Road station. As children we used to marvel at these huge machines as they came in from Cricklewood with up to 100

Ex-works and commendably clean, 8F 2-8-0 No.48671 stands alongside the ash lifting plant, a lightly built structure akin to the coaler in terms of its remoteness from mainstream LMS practice. Two features to notice are, in the distance, the wagon tippler for up-ending wagons of coal for the elevator plant and, to the right, the local wagon repair shop. Photograph K.C.H. Fairey.

46137 THE PRINCE OF WALES'S VOLUNTEERS SOUTH LANCASHIRE stands on the shed yard in front of the water softener, with the wheel drop building to the right, 28th April 1960. Royal Scots were unusual at 15A and only appeared, generally, if in need of minor attention. Just before I took this picture the Assistant DMPS made a suggestion to improve the final result, handing me some chalk to whiten up the shed plate. So beware bright white plates! Photograph K.C.H. Fairey.

coal empties. I suppose some of the old railwaymen could look aghast at the length of the aggregate trains hauled nowadays by the Class 59s on the Western Region lines!

There were twice daily iron ore workings to the NER from London Road, with an extensive standard gauge quarry system feeding the exchange sidings, served by a variety of industrial tank locomotives. There was also a metre gauge system, which went under the Midland main line near Finedon Road Signal Box to bring iron ore from the Finedon Quarries direct to Wellingborough Furnaces, situated nearby on the down side of the main line. Fortunately all three metre gauge 0-6-0Ts survive and are in process of being returned to full working order at the Irchester Railway Museum.

13th September 1956, and 48005 together with other 8Fs and 2-10-0s, awaits its turn of duty, resting in the shed yard. This is the view from the footpath, showing in the background the wheeldrop, the old repair shop and, on the right, the fitters' shop adjoining No.2 shed. Photograph K.C.H. Fairey.

An immaculate BR 4MT 2-6-4T retires to the 'halfway house' of Wellingborough, returning to the Tilbury Section after a visit to Derby, 29th June 1961. Photograph K.C.H. Fairey.

No.85 has been completed and looks very smart in lined green livery. Standard gauge train loads of ore were also received from time to time from the north, necessitating several movements to get from the up slow line across the main lines and reverse again into the Furnace Sidings. These were normally hauled by Stanier 8Fs or 9F 2-10-0s.

When 9F 2-10-0s Nos.92008 and 92009 came new to Wellingborough early in 1954 they were readily accepted by the men - in fact as more came into the district Leicester frequently used them successfully on Saturday excursions and extras. It was a very different story when

1st July 1962. Four 2-6-4Ts, unusual visitors to Wellingborough, drop in on their way to Derby from the London area. Photograph K.C.H. Fairey.

A varied group clustered around the turntable in No.2 shed, taking a well-earned Sunday rest, 10th June 1962. Several of our locos were absent at weekends and visitors from other depots always enlivened the scene. Photograph K.C.H. Fairey.

Wellingborough was saddled with not one Crosti boilered version 2-10-0 but the whole batch of ten! The exhaust from the side mounted chimney soon found its way into the cabs and very little improvement seems to have come from a smoke deflector modification. Added to this were the later problems of pre-heater boiler corrosion so a sigh of relief went up when they were laid aside for conversion to a more or less standard 2-10-0. The first to be done was 92026 and as time went by the class moved to different parts of the system.

A Coalville engine, 2F No.58148, inside No.2 shed after undergoing piston and valve examination, 6th May 1962. It's obvious from the hardware laying about that No.2 was the shed where repairs took place. Photograph K.C.H. Fairey.

Looking back at Wellingborough then one can only dream of the 'good old days' of the late 'fifties and early 'sixties. HSTs have revolutionised the passenger service - the endless procession of coal trains are but a memory and if it were not for the aggregate workings to and from Leicester and the occasional ballast and engineering trains there would be no freight movements at all. So slip back with me to the 'fifties and 'sixties at Wellingborough, where an unmistakable pall of smoke hung about the great vaulting roofs of the roundhouses, and the rattle and clatter of wagons was ceaseless...

Right : 1st June 1960, and Wellingborough receives an unusual visitor, V2 60863 of Leicester Central shed. Until later years this class was never seen at Wellingborough but Leicester Central V2s made regular appearances for heavy repairs, once the shed came under LMR control. Photograph K.C.H. Fairey.

One of Wellingborough's unloved Crosti-boilered 2-10-0s, No.92028, making up a coal train for London, on 16th July 1959. The engine is standing on the Up Slow, with Neilsons Sidings behind the signals and Henlow Sidings on the far right. The two turnouts on the far left lead to Wellingborough Furnaces and this picture demonstrates the complicated access for any Up Slow line trains. They had to draw forward, set back on to the Down Slow and then move forward again, crossing both Up and Down main lines and finally propelling the train into the furnaces. Photograph K.C.H. Fairey.

Above : 92028 passing No.2 shed on an up coal train on 31st May 1957, about to go under Mill Road bridge. Innumerable were the occasions when, as trainspotting children, we would cross the bridge, creep down the path leading to the roundhouse and peep inside... to ordered back by the fitters. Photograph K.C.H. Fairey.

Below : 92029 takes a Christmas rest on the shed yard, 28th December 1958. This is the perfect viewpoint to note the smoke deflector modifications and the pre-heating boiler, slung under the conventional one. Photograph K.C.H. Fairey.

Above : 13th August 1959, and the Crostis are in store awaiting conversion. These two curiously remote roads at the east side of No.2 shed had previously served to store the Garratts at weekends. Photograph K.C.H. Fairey.

Below : 92026, the first Crosti to be converted, posed in the sun outside No.1 shed on 25th October 1959. With this a Sunday, the Running Foreman was not best pleased at my request to move 92026 into a better position for photography. As you can see, fortunately he relented! Photograph K.C.H. Fairey.

Left : A memory of earlier days - Garratt No.47969 struggles over the River Nene bridge (on the loop from London Road station to the Midland main line) with an afternoon ore train to the north east, 26th May 1957. These trains were a source of great annoyance to road users at the A45 London Road level crossing. The 48 wagons of ore had to be propelled across the roadway and with a muffled roar the giant Garratt would move forward, the crew hoping for a flying start up the heavily graded loop to the Midland line. Many was the fist shaken (and many the muttered, or not so muttered, curse directed, I fancy) at the crew by frustrated and delayed motorists as the train made its slow progress across the main road. Photograph K.C.H. Fairey.

Right : Claud 4-4-0 No.62613 from Peterborough (Spital Bridge - ex-Midland shed) heads the afternoon train to Northampton at Wellingborough London Road. No trace of the station now remains and the level crossing has long since gone - in fact the new dual carriageway A45 road bridge now occupies the same spot and the road in the picture runs simply between Wellingborough and Newport Pagnell. Photograph K.C.H. Fairey.

Above : Black 5 No.45324 arrives at London Road station with the afternoon local from Peterborough East to Northampton. The loop up to the Midland leaves this line just beyond the signal box in the distance. The iron ore exchange sidings were on the right and the tracks on the left went to Messrs. Whitworth's flour mill and silo. Photograph K.C.H. Fairey.

Below : Endpiece. Poignant conjunction of an 8F and the rapidly disappearing No.1 roundhouse, 2nd July 1964. Photograph K.C.H. Fairey.

WAR REPORT
Kings Cross, 11th May 1940

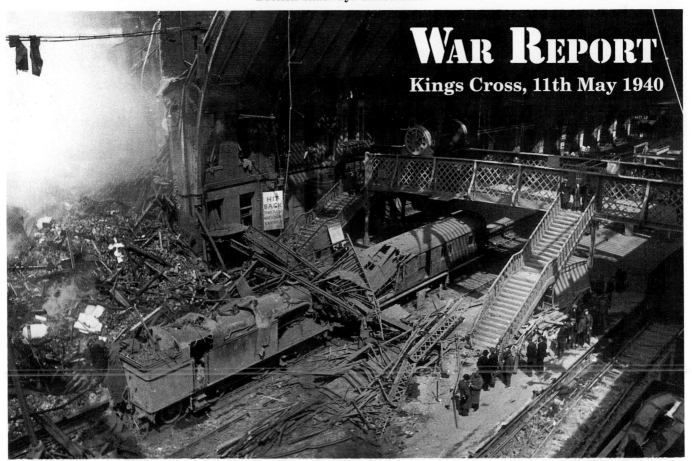

Bombs fell in the vicinity of Kings Cross station on the night of 10th-11th May 1940, though the main casualty was the booking office. Two staff miraculously escaped serious injury, but millions of tickets were incinerated or utterly dispersed. An account of the affair in the *LNER Magazine* runs: *"In pitch darkness, the two men made their escape from the wreckage, and then, badly shaken and with clothes torn, sat down for a while to consider how they should carry on the work, which had been so suddenly interrupted. Apparently they decided that the passengers for the next train must be booked somehow, though even they could not shut their eyes to the fact that the virtual disappearance of their office and all that was in it presented some difficulty. However there was another office near by, very much smaller and not equipped with the requisite tickets, and with no staff on duty. They decided to install themselves there. They scoured surrounding offices for excess ticket books and blank cards, and, with the aid of the staff who came on duty later, the first morning train was successfully booked."* HIT BACK says the poster!

Principal victim, N2 0-6-2T No.4761. It is standing at Platform 10, looking as dazed as any inanimate thing can look; it survived the experience and was afterwards dragged out and back to Kings Cross shed. It was eventually put back in order and was not finally withdrawn until 1960.

Left : Smoking debris at Platform 10, entirely obscuring the N2.

Middle : The wreckage had largely been cleared by the end of May, and though Platform 10 road was clear, it was occupied by wagons taking away the debris. Once any dangerous girdering and brickwork had been taken down, a vast gap was left at Kings Cross, which the knowledgeable, from minor discontinuities in the ironwork, can still discern today. This is the temporary arrangement of crude shelters, made of old rail, in April 1942.

Bottom : Preliminary work (LNER crane in attendance) in restoring the glorious Kings Cross roofing, 17th November 1946. We are lucky that the station was restored as it was - discussions as to how the replacement might proceed threw up some hair-raising schemes, including one allowing for 'future air traffic'! Proposals for a concrete roof mercifully came to nought, as did a plan to replicate the LMS station at Leeds City...

CORNISH RIVIERA EXPRESS

A Silver Anniversary - Building the Cornish Riviera Express

Thirties File is a regular feature of *British Railways Illustrated* and for this example we cheat ever so slightly - new stock for the famous train was constructed in 1929 and completed in time for the summer that year, going into service from Monday 8th July 1929. The new train, the GWR publicity announced, included vehicles having:

"Improved Features of Design and Increased Allowances of Passenger Space, in Celebration of the 25th Anniversary of the Inauguration of this World-Famous Train"

In 1929 it was indeed twenty five years since the Cornish Riviera had been inaugurated, booked to run the 225.7 miles (it had been 246 in 1904) non-stop, and early in 1929 it was determined that a suitable time had come for the sets of vehicles which had been placed in service on the train at different times since its beginning to be replaced. There were to be new sets, embodying the most up-to-date improvements. The running of these 'Silver Anniversary' vehicles coincided with the resumption of non-stop running between London and Plymouth,

on an accelerated schedule of four hours for that section.

During the summer months the train included only one slip portion, detached at Westbury for Yeovil and Weymouth, for the heavy holiday traffic meant that there were other trains for this - through the rest of the year there were Taunton and Exeter slip portions. The new train described here, as in the original *Railway Gazette* notes, is thus the summer make-up - the Plymouth and Penzance section could be reduced in winter by two or three ordinary vehicles in compensation for Taunton and Exeter slip portions, similar to that of the Weymouth coach. The standard composition of the complete train as run during the summer, was announced in July 1929 as follows in the table below.

Above : Brake 3rd. Sliding ventilators were later fitted, altering the external look of the vehicles greatly. They were withdrawn during 1957-62.

	Vehicle	No. of comp.	No. of pass.	Tare	Destination
1	Brake third	2	16	32t 10c	Penzance
2	Third	8	64	34t 3c	Penzance
3	Third	8	64	34t 3c	Penzance
4	Third dining saloon	-	64	32t 11c	Penzance
5	Kitchen car	-	-	42t 13c	Penzance
6	First and third dining saloon	-	24 1st, 31 3rd	32t 17c	Penzance
7	First and third composite	4,3	24 1st, 24 3rd	34t 3c	Penzance
8	Brake third	2	16	32t 10c	Penzance
9	First and third brake composite	2,4	12 1st, 32 3rd	34t 5c	St Ives
10	First and third brake composite	2,4	12 1st, 32 3rd	34t 5c	Falmouth
11	First and third brake composite	2,4	12 1st, 32 3rd	34t 5c	Det. at Plymouth
12	Double-ended slip	2,4	12 1st, 32 3rd	36t 6c	Weymouth
13	First and third brake composite	2,4	12 1st, 32 3rd	34t 5c	Weymouth

Above : Construction of the coaches under way in May 1929 - an indication of the speed of the building process. This is the floor of a Kitchen Car - Seating (see table) amounted to 428 in the compartments, while the accommodation of the restaurant cars was for 119 passengers, 24 first class and 95 third class. The publicity claimed that 'never more than two meal sittings are required to serve all the passengers desiring (restaurant) accommodation'. As far as novel features were concerned, interest centred principally upon the Kitchen Car, as *The Railway Gazette* relates - it had the same general dimensions as other vehicles and thus provided much more extensive accommodation than had been usual with previous kitchen cars. A feature considered of great note was that at each end there was 'a lavatory compartment for the use of passengers, this being, however, well away from the kitchen car accommodation proper'.

Middle above : Slip Composite under construction, 25th May 1929, a view showing the side framing and the fascinating interlacing network of beaming. Does *any* construction process now employ such a level and intensity of specialised skill, with so many practitioners concentrated together? The Cornish Riviera Express was, like all its contemporaries, from the grandest saloon to the humblest workmen's carriage, hand built.

Left : Woodworking Masterclass. Lifting the side of a Dining Saloon, ready for its emplacement, 18th May 1929.

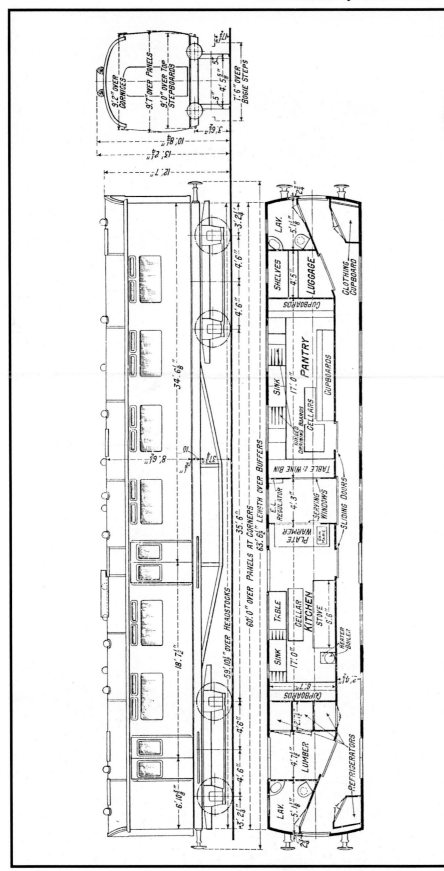

Above : 10th June 1929, and carriages of the Silver Anniversary Cornish Riviera approach completion.

Right : Interior of 1st Class Dining Car, its sumptuous seating arranged for four passengers per table one side and two at the other. The peculiar mark in the centre of the image is not some nameless stain - perish the thought - but a blemish on the negative. Which is something we can surely overlook, given that the print is now more than 65 years old...

Kitchen Car - above. It was found desirable to provide lavatories separate from those in the compartment coaches. Next to the lavatory at each end of the Kitchen Cars was a general purpose section, in one case in the form of a 'lumber' room in which the stewards could place hampers and other supplies not needed until later in the journey, while the corresponding compartment at the other end was available for passengers' luggage which might be brought to the dining saloon. The two main sections are the kitchen and the pantry, each 17ft. long and 6ft. 7in. wide. Between them is a stewards' section 4ft. 3in. wide enabling waiters to obtain what they need either from the kitchen or from the pantry through serving windows on each side. This was found to be a great advantage, in that waiters attending at the service windows did not occupy space in the corridor and could thus 'pursue their duties without interfering with passengers passing through the corridor or with other waiters or train staff'. The kitchen was equipped with Fletcher Russell cooking stove, water heater, plate warmer and bain marie, the equipment being completed by cupboards, sink, table etc. as necessary. There was a plate warmer for 400 plates, a soup warmer and, in the corridor at one corner, a refrigerating plant. There were also refrigerator compartments for storing fish, meat and 'sealed bottles of milk'. At the end of the vehicle at the corner alongside the corridor, was a clothing cupboard for use by the kitchen staff. Both the kitchen and pantry had 'cellars' for wine, duly fitted *into the floor*. The kitchen car was lined throughout with stainless steel sheets.

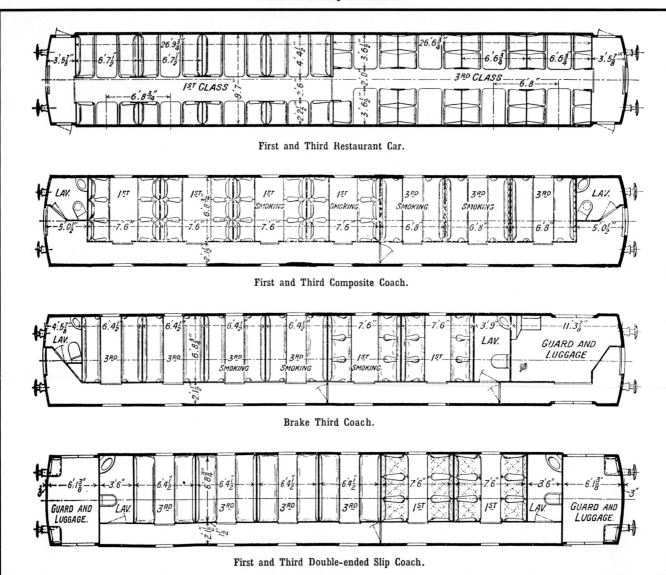

First and Third Restaurant Car.

First and Third Composite Coach.

Brake Third Coach.

First and Third Double-ended Slip Coach.

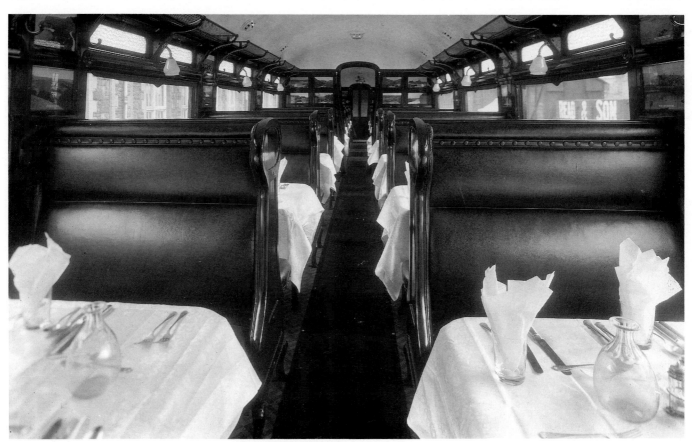

More austere, yet still by no means uninviting, 3rd Class dining.

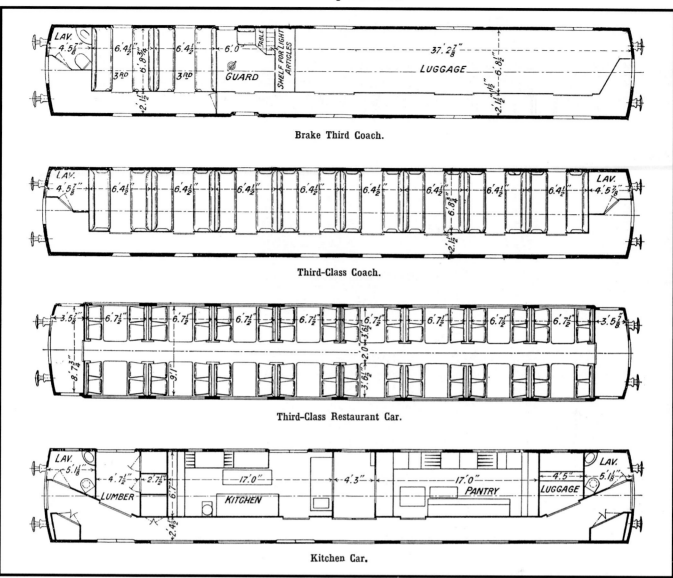

Brake Third Coach.

Third-Class Coach.

Third-Class Restaurant Car.

Kitchen Car.

Above : Kitchen interior.

Right : 1st Class compartment. 'One of the special features' of the new trains (though it severely inhibited their usefulness in later years, when the authorities tried to put them to use elsewhere) was an increase in space for every passenger. The vehicles had a maximum width of 9ft. 7in. over handles, so that the compartments had widths of up to 6ft. 8in. for 3rd Class (in some instances - most were three and a half inches less) and 7ft. 6in. 1st Class.

Left : 3rd Class interior.

Right : 3rd Class compartment, with a gloriously faked town 'somewhere in the shires' outside the window.

Left : 1st class view, again 'doctored' for effect. The reality of the outside was probably a brick wall at Swindon.

Below : Kitchen Car.

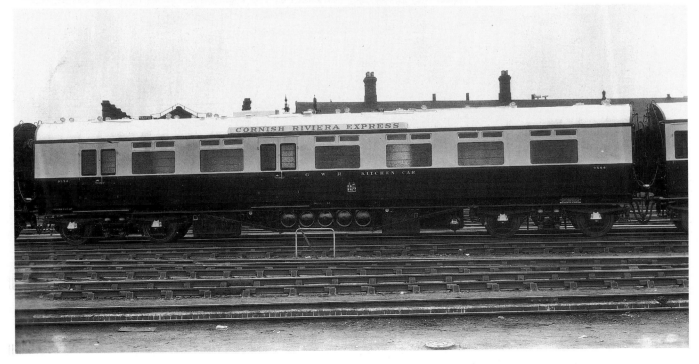

Top : 1st and 3rd Class Restaurant Car. Glass fitted into the steel panels so as to lie practically flush, avoiding the more elaborate panelling previously used. Lighting throughout was electric, and the usual Great Western standard systems of steam heating, ventilation and so on were provided.

Middle : 3rd Class Restaurant Car.

Bottom : 1st and 3rd Class Composite Coach. This new stock built in 1929-30, Harris records, was for the Torbay Express and the principal Paddington - West of England expresses as well as the Cornish Riviera; the vehicles were distinguished by a red triangle at each end, and GWR *Rules* stipulated that they were restricted to specific routes: from Paddington to Penzanze via Westbury or Bristol, to Fishguard, Neyland and Milford Haven and to Wolverhampton.

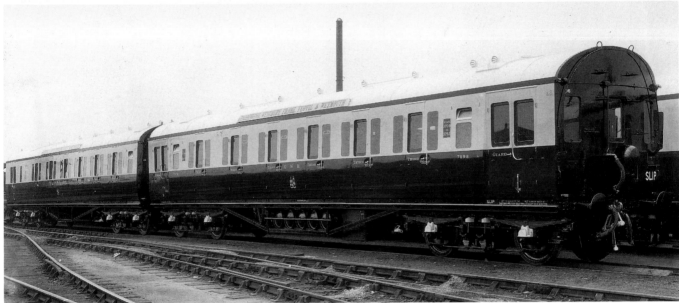

Top : 3rd Class Coach. The stock was heavy and had 9ft. bogies, at a time when 7ft was a standard. The Vita glass was considered worthy of note in the original *Railway Gazette* description of 1929, and Harris has unearthed further references to it in the GWR *Cheltenham Flyer* booklet of six years later - apparently a principal virtue was its property of admitting 'health giving ultra violet rays', which normal glass, it seems, excluded...

Middle : The 1st/3rd Brake Composite together with double ended Slip Coach. The total weight of the train, including the slip portion, was 448 tons 16cwt, of which 378 tons 5 cwt had to be taken over the very severe gradients between Newton Abbot and Plymouth (North Road).

Bottom : 1st, 3rd Brake Composite. In order to secure the enlarged dimensions it was necessary to provide recesses in the outside panelling for the door handles - a feature excellently illustrated here.

FOURUM
Summer goings-on at Malton

B1 No.61069 on the 10.50am Scarborough - Newcastle, 29th July 1961. The B1 is on the line (this piece could be designed to send readers, dazedly, for their *Atlas/Gazeteers* - what a pity Irwell Press doesn't publish one) from Scarborough which runs south westwards to York and with its train has just passed under a line running west - east, from, on the East Coast main line, to Driffield in remote East Riding. West to east is, roughly, left to right in this view. The B1 wants to take its train up on to that line, westwards (to the left) to gain the ECML for the onward run to Newcastle - that is, it needs to go to the left. There is, however, no curve for the purpose; the only curve runs *eastward*, seen to the *right* in this view. So, the train has to reverse up the curve to the right and for this purpose it needs to run forward (that is, southwards) from where we see it here, past the photographer and virtually into Malton station, which lies behind the photographer, in order to reverse.

To gain the curve and the line west to Pilmoor the train, on reversing, has briefly to head east; another engine has to come on the rear and guide it up the curve - in this instance, Ivatt 2-6-2T No.41247. The train now, it will be noted, has moved a further road across - it is now on the curve, as if it were going east to Driffield. However - another complication - the line to Driffield had closed in 1958 and no longer existed a short distance beyond the junction with the curve. It was known as Scarborough Road Junction - a bit of the old line was retained for trains to get on and reverse, but little more.

So, the train, headed by 41247, has now got up on to the remnant of the Driffield line and is ready to head off west with 61069 at its head - 41247 is now at the tail. It might help in visualising all this to know that the bridge underneath the train is that seen above the train in the *first* photograph, opposite page top - the train is now at a right angle to its position in that first photo.

Another bridge, this time over the River Derwent. The train has set off behind the B1 and the Ivatt tank is dropping off, its task complete, ready to go back light to Malton. This bridge is a little to the west of the bridge in the previous photo and the first photo: the photographer has simply swung round to his left to capture the last of a fascinating series of manoeuvres. *All photographs P.B. Booth, Neville Stead Collection.*

FOURUM

An Early Channel Crossing

The Channel Tunnel, Marvel of the Age though it assuredly must be, is hardly an appropriate subject for *British Railways Illustrated*. The magazine, not to say its illustrious *Annuals* and *Summer Specials*, would grow dizzy and reach for some restorative salts at such an unsettling intrusion of gross modernity. A fine folding album in the possession of John Tatchell, however, reveals something of earlier French links, quite a bit different in character from the electrified gliding smoothness of today...

Calais, Maritime. The ship in the first photograph, above, is carrying Superintendents and Goods Managers of the Railway Clearing House, for their conference in Paris, in July 1900, and this second photograph is obviously a record of the arrival at Calais - though quite which ship is which, is unclear. The nearest vessel is EXPRESS but it is not EXPRESS which is shown above.

The Superintendents and Goods Managers it appears, took their wives on the trip, and the set of four souvenir photos (the date is given no more precisely than 'July 1900') was not of course complete without the group shot...

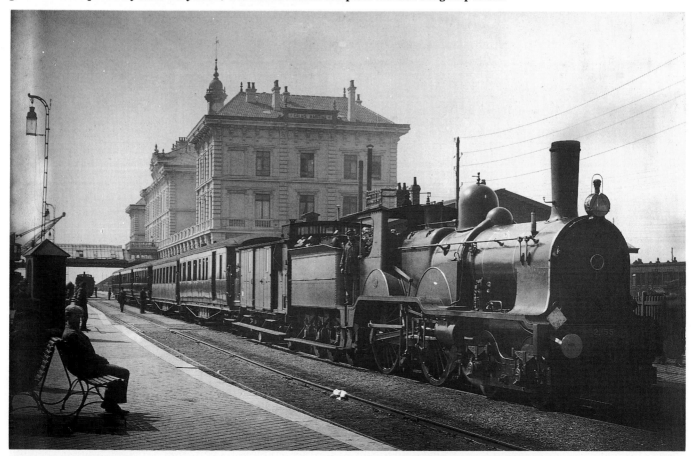

The party's train ready for departure from Calais Maritime - presumably bound for Paris and the RCH conference. The conversation of passengers doubtless at whiles turned to the dream of a Channel tunnel, and doubtless the demise of the Railway Clearing House was foreseen only dimly at the least, if at all. Now the Tunnel has at last come into its inheritance, and the hoops through which our railway organisation is now being forced recall to many minds nothing so much as a re-invention of the RCH...

To most non-locals, Somerset is the land of cider, cheese and a cricket club which seems over-acquainted with that modern-day concept, 'self destruction'. To railway enthusiasts, however, the county's appeal was somewhat different. Somerset offered scope, it is true, for unusual underlinings in three of the four major sections in the Ian Allan *Combined Volume* (WR, SR and LMR - many of them 'exotics') while the more serious student, maybe, concerned with the bucolic delights of the English rural branch, was spoiled for choice.

Of all the branch lines in Somerset, the longest was that between Yatton, on the Bristol - Exeter main line and

Witham on the Reading - Westbury - Taunton line, an extraordinary *near-thirty two miles* of rural ride. The term 'classic GWR country branch' is, perhaps, an over-employed one, but in the case of the Yatton - Witham route it is unarguably appropriate. The line served, among other places, Wells and Cheddar - both well-known for their many attractions - but although it accommodated tourist traffic, it was primarily a year-round means of transportation for locals. Furthermore, the line handled a significant amount of traffic from the local quarries, and it is the stone from one of these which has resulted in part of the branch remaining open to this day.

One element of the branch's appeal was, in true West Country fashion, the local scenery. A section of the route crossed the rugged Mendip Hills, and another section ran alongside their southern slopes. The Mendips were lyrically described by Maxwell Fraser in his book *Somerset*, written in 1934 as a publicity vehicle for the GWR: '*The mysterious fascination of the Mendips is so real and vital to those who know this extraordinary upland, that it seems as though the hills are a living entity... It is only in the solitary heart of the plateau that the queer spirit of Mendip is made manifest. Those who keep to the great highways, or the network of roads linking the innumerable villages on Mendip never fully sense the strange wild soul of the hills, but these Mendip villages have such a compelling fascination that they are in themselves a little world of beauty and interest, while the vast gorges and caves they neighbour have an added quality of rarity which is irresistible*'. Heady stuff indeed.

The Railway is Born
The Yatton - Witham branch was built in two distinctly separate parts and, moreover, by two distinctly separate companies. The proverbial seed was

By Martin Smith

The Standard 3MT 2-6-2Ts made their debut on the Cheddar Valley/East Somerset line in 1958, and were still there at the end of the passenger era. No.82039 pulls away from Shepton Mallet with the 3.28pm Witham - Yatton train on 27th July 1963; the station was suffixed 'High Street' on 26th September 1949, the nearby ex-S&D station distinguished by the suffix 'Charlton Road' at the same time. PHOTOGRAPH HUGH BALLANTYNE.

Table 79 — YATTON, CHEDDAR, WELLS and WITHAM

Miles	Week Days	am	am	am (Except Sats.)	am (Saturdays only)	pm (Sats. only)	am (Except Saturdays)	pm (Except Sats.)	pm (Sats. only)	pm	pm (Except Sats.)	pm	pm	Sundays pm	Sundays pm
	61 Bristol (T. Meads). dep	..	7 25	9 0	1012	..	10 40	..	1240	2Y 0	5 20	5 50	7 30	2 10	..
—	Yatton .... dep	6 55	7 58	9 35	1112		11 35		1 10	2 52 V	5 47	6 10	8 8	2 30	
1¼	Congresbury	7 0	8 3	9 40	1116		11 39		1 14	2 55	5 50	6 14	8 12	2 34	
4¼	Sandford and Banwell	7 6	8 9	9 46	1122		11 45		1 20	3 1	5 56	6 20	8 18	2 40	
5¾	Winscombe (Somerset)	7 10	8 13	9 50	1126		11 50		1 24	3 5	6 0	6 24	8 22	2 44	
8	Axbridge	7 15	8 20	9 55	1130		11 54		1 29	3 11	6 5	6 29	8 27	2 49	
9½	Cheddar	7 20	8 26	10 0	1135		12 0		1 34	3 18	6 10	6 34	8 32	2 54	
12	Draycott	7 27	8 31	10 5	1140		12 3		1 39	3 22	6 14	6 39	8 37	2 58	
14	Lodge Hill	7 32	8 36	1010	1145		12 8		1 44	3 28	6 19	6 44	8 42	..	
16¼	Wookey	7 37	8 41	1015	1150		12 13		1 49	3 32	6 24	6 49	8 47	3 7	
17½	Wells arr	7 40	8 44	1019	1153		12 17		1 53	3 36	6 28	6 52	8 50	3 10	
	Wells dep		8 56			12 3		1230		3 49		7 0			4 0
22¾	Shepton Mallet D		9 10			1218		1245		4 4		7 16			4 15
26	Cranmore		9 19			1226		1253		4 14		7 24			4 23
29¼	Wanstrow		9 26			1233		1 0		4 21		7 31			4 30
31¾	Witham arr		9 31			1239		1 5		4 26		7 36			4 36

Miles	Week Days	am	am	am	am (Except Sats.)	am S	pm S	pm E	pm (Sats. only)	pm E	pm S	pm (Except Sats.)	pm	pm	pm	Sundays pm	Sundays pm
	Witham dep	..	..	8 23		1010	1 10	1 30		3 30	3 37		6 52	..	9 20	5 40	..
2½	Wanstrow			8 30		1017	1 16	1 36		3 38	3 45		7 0		9 28	5 46	
5¾	Cranmore			8 37		1027	1 23	1 43		3 46	3 53		7 8		9 38	5 53	
9	Shepton Mallet D			8 44		1034	1 31	1 53		4B 3	4 3		7 16		9 46	6 3	
14¼	Wells arr			8 54		1045	1 42	2 2		4 12	4 12		7 26		9 57	6 14	
	Wells dep	7 5	8 0	9 5	1035	1110	1 55	2 5	2 46	4 17	4 22	7 0		8 15			7 20
15¼	Wookey	7 8	8 3	9 8	1038	1113	1 57	2 8	2 49	4 19	4 25	7 3		8 18			7 23
17¾	Lodge Hill	7 13	8 8	9 13	1043	1118	2 2	2 13	2 54	4 24	4 30	7 8		8 23			
19¾	Draycott	7 17	8 12	9 17	1047	1122	2 6	2 19	2 58	4 30	4 34	7 13		8 27			7 33
22	Cheddar	7 21	8 16	9 21	1052	1126	2 10	2 25	3 3	4 37	4 40	7 18		8 32			7 38
23¾	Axbridge	7 25	8 22	9 26	1056	1130	2 15	2 31	3 10	4 44	4 44	7 23		8 36			7 43
26	Winscombe (Somerset)	7 30	8 27	9 31	11 1	1137	2 20	2 36	3 15	4 49	4 49	7 29		8 41			7 49
27½	Sandford and Banwell	7 33	8 30	9 34	11 4	1140	2 24	2 39	3 18	4 52	4 52	7 33		8 44			7 54
30½	Congresbury	7 38	8 35	9 40	1110	1146	2 30	2 44	3 23	4 58	4 58	7 40		8 52			8 0
31¾	Yatton arr	7 42	8 39	9 44	1115	1150	2 36	2 49	3 28	5 6	5 2	7 47		8 58			8 4
43¾	61 Bristol (T. Meads).. arr	8 16	9 11	10 8	1148	1215	3 2	3 16	4 1	5 36	5 36	8 11		9 51			8 25

B Arr 3 54 pm
D High Street Station; about 1 mile to Charlton Road Station

E Except Saturdays
S Saturdays only

V Third class only, Mondays to Fridays. First and Third class on Saturdays
Y First and Third class. Dep 2 15 pm on Saturdays

Summer 1955 services on the Wells branch. Mention is made of the former S&D station at Shepton Mallet but passenger services over the old S&D into Priory Road station at Wells ceased in 1951.

sown on 5th June 1856 when the East Somerset Railway was formally incorporated to construct a nine and a half mile line from Witham to Shepton Mallet. The ESR had originally planned to build on a completely new alignment between Frome and Shepton Mallet, but after its engineer - Brunel - had assessed the cost of carving the route, the company had adopted the cheaper option of linking up with the ex-Wilts, Somerset & Weymouth line at Witham.

A working agreement with the GWR meant that the East Somerset Railway was built to the broad gauge. Enough land was acquired to permit doubling at a future date and the bridges were constructed with this in mind, but the line was to remain single. Opening was dependent upon Board of Trade approval of the construction and operation, and the record of these examinations is a principal, often the only, insight into the state of many lines as

2MT 2-6-2T No.41245 arrives at Cheddar with the 3.28pm Witham to Yatton train on 17th August 1963. The locomotive wears the 82E shedplate of Bristol Barrow Road, Bath Road depot having, by then, closed to steam. PHOTOGRAPH HUGH BALLANTYNE.

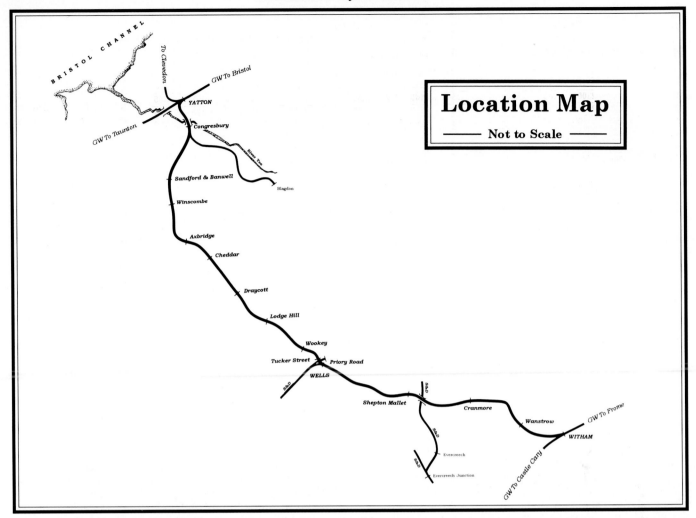

they began life. Colonel Yolland was in charge of the inspection on 29th October 1858, recording that sidings were provided 'only at the extremities' of the line, and that there were nineteen bridges on the line, '11 under and eight over, the whole of which with the exception of one over-bridge are built of stone with lime mortar.' Colonel Yolland recorded that there was a turn-

table at Shepton Mallet, but not at the junction at Witham Friary. There were only two stations - Cranmore and Shepton Mallet.

Although there were only these two stations to start with, a basic platform was later opened at Wanstrow, the cost of its construction being borne by the villagers. It has been suggested that the platform opened in 1860, but offi-

cial GWR records give a date of April 1909. In view of the fact that a station master was appointed (by the GWR) at Wanstrow in April 1909, and in the apparent absence of further details, could it be that the platform was nominally *owned* by the villagers until 1909? Whatever the case, until the 1920s Wanstrow station consisted of little more than a platform; arrange-

North British diesel-hydraulic No.D6342 pulls into Cheddar with the 10.49 (SO) Witham -Yatton on 17th August 1963. The tail of the eastbound 11.12 (SO) is just about visible in the station. PHOTOGRAPH HUGH BALLANTYNE.

CHEDDAR																	
	Staff		Passenger Traffic			Goods Traffic											
Year	Total	Wages £	Tickets		Receipts total £	Forwarded (tons)			Received (tons)			coal not charged (tons)	goods total		livet'k (vans)	Total rec. £
			issued	season		coal	mins.	gen.	coal	mins.	gen.		tons	rec. £		
1903	8	424	30750	?	4774	8	11169	1814	3158	1375	5561	1239	24324	6123	274	10897
1913	7	489	25294	?	4598	-	426	1080	1484	408	3180	1414	7992	2831	150	7429
1923	9	1380	23001	160	6599	10	3545	4149	2325	1962	3432	3515	18938	10686	151	17285
1924	10	1291	20433	131	6146	56	7218	7118	2957	1059	3255	5285	26948	14478	123	20624
1925	9	1462	21535	130	5585	72	8667	10641	2132	1318	3746	6934	33510	17448	173	23033
1926	9	1383	16507	139	4758	9	11416	13270	1361	601	3006	5110	34773	16810	144	21568
1927	11	1802	17914	118	5078	32	21850	15229	2032	639	2959	5914	48655	23793	124	28871
1928	12	1848	16050	143	4658	-	17408	13211	1877	913	2890	5572	41871	20808	132	25466
1929	12	1915	13557	119	4263	-	21759	16501	2181	1584	2873	3139	48037	25502	131	29765
1930	12	1953	9777	91	3371	-	12311	14293	1822	474	4386	2713	35999	21261	65	24632
1931	12	1752	8509	96	3139	-	17319	12522	1743	283	2333	2541	36741	19528	20	22667
1932	11	1615	7372	109	2631	-	36677	9291	1765	348	2056	2483	52620	24586	12	27217
1933	11	1785	8139	150	2700	-	57702	8829	1352	1561	5414	5228	80086	35458	6	38158

changing carriages at Witham Friary, then as there is a Turntable at Frome, the one at Shepton Mallet will suffice'.

Due to the ill-considered turntable arrangements, Colonel Yolland declined to recommend that the line be opened. The ESR had originally intended to work the line with tender engines, but in the light of his comments tank engines were used instead. The change of policy was preferable to either the capital expenditure on a second turntable or working through to and from Frome - it also allowed the line to be opened. For the ceremonial opening on 9th November 1858, the locomotive was GWR 'Bogie'

ments were only expanded it seems, after 1925, the GWR Traffic Committee minutes for 29 October noting: *'WANSTROW - provision of accommodation for goods and livestock, £1,260. APPROVED'.* The facilities were officially brought into use in January 1927.

recommend that the maximum speed should not be permitted to exceed 30 miles an hour'. (The approach to Wanstrow from the east required a climb of 1 in 47 while, to the west of Wanstrow, gradients reached 1 in 54).

There was nothing too much out of the ordinary in all this, but Colonel Yolland expressed concern about the arrangements (or the lack of them) for working the line:

'I understand that the line is to be worked by the Great Western Railway Company, but I am not in possession of the regulations under which it is proposed to be worked. As it is a single line, and as it joins another single line at Witham Friary, unusual care will be required in framing the regulations, and if it is to be worked separately from the Junction a Turntable is required there, or the one put up at Shepton Mallet will be useless. If it is to be worked through to Frome, instead of

class 4-4-0ST HOMER. When public services commenced, they comprised five trains each way.

At Witham - where the ESR diverged from the Frome to Castle Cary line - the main line through the station was, at the time, single track, doubling not being undertaken until 1881. The ESR trains used the up side of the station but, as the bay here had no run-round loop, reversing manoeuvres had to be undertaken by gravity shunting - similar to the procedure employed for example, at Yelverton (the junction for the Princetown branch) and Maiden Newton (for the Bridport branch).

The main line at Witham took on increased significance in 1906 when the

The main station in England's smallest city was hardly a grand affair. On 31st August 1963 pannier tank No.3696 waits at Tucker Street with the 3.28pm Witham - Yatton train. PHOTOGRAPH HUGH BALLANTYNE.

Returning to Col. Yolland's inspection report, he was generally satisfied but nevertheless noted that:

'Distant signals in both directions on the Wilts Somerset & Weymouth Branch (the Frome - Castle Cary line) are required at the Junction at Witham Friary, and one is required at Shepton Mallet station.

'There is no lodge at the authorized Level Crossing.... The end of the platform at Shepton Mallet is to be ramped off.... Gradient Boards have not been put up.... As there are very heavy gradients, and sharp S curves without any intervening straight portions, I would

2-6-2T No.41245, in the branch bay at Yatton with the 1.45pm for Wells, witnesses a sad event on 7th September 1963 - the last scheduled steam-hauled 9.45 Paddington to Weston-super-Mare train, arriving in the charge of 7036 (numberplate gone) TAUNTON CASTLE. PHOTOGRAPH HUGH BALLANTYNE.

GWR unveiled its new cut-off route through south Somerset to Taunton, West Country expresses subsequently being re-routed via Witham and the new cut-off. That, however, did not elevate the status of Witham, as the expresses to Devon and Cornwall did not deign to stop at the little rural station.

Even before the ESR had opened, a vociferous lobby from Wells had pressed for the railway to be extended to its city. The East Somerset Railway gained authorisation for a five mile extension to Wells in July 1857, but construction was delayed by a change of contractor. In the meantime, a horse bus service was provided between Shepton Mallet station and Wells.

The Wells extension was eventually completed, but did not wholly satisfy the BoT's inspector - again, Colonel Yolland. He required that a turntable be installed at Wells and that the 'table at Shepton Mallet be transferred to Witham. The ESR agreed to attend to the matter, and also undertook to install an electric telegraph, for by then, the 'one engine in steam' arrangement was proving to be a great handicap. Subject to those undertakings, permission to open the extension was granted. The formal opening took place on 28th February 1862, and the serious business of extracting money from fare-paying passengers commenced the following day, 1st March.

The Wells extension included gradients even more ferocious than those on the Witham - Shepton Mallet section - leaving Wells, trains had to ne-

gotiate a climb of 1 in 46. At Wells, the ESR station was on the west side of Gate Lane, and consisted of a single platform with a glass awning. A level crossing carried the railway across Gate Lane where there was a small goods shed in the yard on the north side of the running line. On the south side was a fifty-foot long single-road engine shed, beyond which was a forty-foot turntable. It is believed that, prior to the opening of the Wells extension, an engine shed had been provided at Shepton Mallet, but the opening of the extension rendered it redundant.

The ESR was not alone in Wells. The Somerset Central Railway's line from Glastonbury to Wells had opened to the public in March 1859 and, almost from the off, had been urged to extend to Shepton Mallet. Fortunately for the East Somerset, the Somerset Central was more absorbed with a possible future link with the Dorset Central Railway. The inevitable merger between the SCR and DCR took place on 1st September 1862, the corporate title for the new concern being the Somerset & Dorset Railway. But we digress....

The ESR was less than a money-spinner. *Bradshaw's Shareholders' Guide* for 1869 revealed that:

'....*notwithstanding the extreme depression of trade during the half-year ending 30 June* (1868), *the returns showed a slight increase over the corresponding period of 1867. The gross earnings for the half-year amounted to £3,582, which after paying £1,033 for interest on debenture debt and rent charges, left £1,530 or 60 per cent of the balance, to the Great Western for working and £1,020 or 40 per cent to the company'.*

The same guide, incidentally, listed the ESR's directors as The Marquis of

Sunny Avon hardly has the ring of *Sunny Somerset*, but this picture was taken on 17th August 1963 and, therefore, long predates the creation of the 'new' synthetic counties. 0-6-0PT No.3702 waits in the branch bay at Yatton with the 2.45pm to Witham. The engine at the goods dock on the right is 0-6-0 No.2268, while the DMU on the far platform awaits its next trip to Clevedon. PHOTOGRAPH HUGH BALLANTYNE.

On the last day of scheduled passenger services at Wells (Tucker Street) - 7th September 1963 - 2268 is in charge of the last eastbound train. Assuming that the train on the left is the last westbound passenger working, the engine would be fellow 0-6-0 No.3218. As evidenced here, the 'last rites' attracted various photographers, but the Cheddar Valley/ East Somerset line seems to have been very well photographed throughout the final summer. PHOTOGRAPH HUGH BALLANTYNE.

Bath (Chairman), whose stately pile was at Longleat, Wilts; James Curtis Somerville (Deputy Chairman) of Dinder House near Wells; Edward Strode of Shepton Mallet; Edmund Clerk of Burford House near Shepton Mallet; Thomas Foxwell of Shepton Mallet; Richard Horner Paget MP of Cranmore Hall; William Berryman of Wells and John Everett, also of Wells.

Competition from the west
The East Somerset Railway was indirectly threatened by the Somerset Central Railway; the latter's line to Wells had originally been worked by the Bristol & Exeter Railway and had, of necessity, been laid with mixed gauge rails. Opting to go it alone in 1861, the SCR's parting with the B&ER had been unusually gentlemanly but nevertheless, when the B&ER later proposed a broad gauge line from Bleadon (to the

south of Weston-super-Mare) and Wells, the SCR's successor, the Somerset & Dorset, felt obliged to promote a competing standard gauge line between Yatton and Wells. The amicability between the two companies seems however to have prevailed, and the B&ER subsequently took over the S&D's plans for the Yatton - Wells route, albeit as a broad gauge line.

In July 1864 the Bristol & Exeter obtained authorisation for the Yatton - Wells branch, nearly eighteen miles, in the name of the Cheddar Valley & Yatton Railway, a nominally independent concern which was formally absorbed by the B&ER in June 1865. The section between Yatton (where a junction was made with the Bristol - Exeter main line) and Cheddar opened on 3rd August 1869, and the line was opened through to Wells on 5th April the following year.

At Wells, it seemed logical that the B&ER should use the East Somerset Railway station, and a draft arrangement was prepared:

'1. The Bristol (& Exeter) Company to be allowed to run all the Passenger Trains except Excursion Trains in and out of the East Somerset Company's Wells Station.

2. The Great Western Company to provide the necessary Staff and perform the services in connection with the Bristol Company's Traffic.

3. The Bristol Company to have the use of the Passenger Station and Sidings for the accommodation of the Engines and Trains, but not Engine Sheds or standing room for spare stock.

4. The Bristol Company to pay the Great Western Company as their proportion of the expenses of the Station a fixed sum of £300 per annum.

5. The Great Western Company to arrange for the working of the gates across the public road dividing the two stations, and the Bristol Company undertaking that they will run no trains into or out of the Station between the hours of 9.30pm and 6.30am.

6. The Bristol Company to pay a nominal rent of £5 to the East Somerset Company for the use of the Station'.

So far so good - but only in theory. The proposed line connecting the B&ER to the ESR passed through the SCR station (Priory Road) and across various SCR sidings on the level. The potential hazards of B&ER passenger trains doing battle with SCR shunting operations caused near apoplexy at the Board of Trade, and permission to ratify the proposed agreement was refused.

Instead of pursuing the matter, the B&ER constructed its own station at Tucker Street, some 600 yards short of the ESR station and 300 yards short of Priory Road station. That might have satisfied the BoT, but it did not amuse the travelling public. The timing of

The relative spaciousness under the roof at Cheddar was partly due to the great breadth demanded by the broad gauge. In this delightfully atmospheric picture, 2-6-2T No.41245 pulls into Cheddar with the 3.28pm Witham - Yatton, on 17th August 1963. PHOTOGRAPH HUGH BALLANTYNE.

On 13th July 1963 Standard 2-6-2Ts Nos.82036 (heading for Yatton) and 82039 (en route for Witham) pass at Shepton Mallet station. PHOTOGRAPH R.E. TOOP.

No.41240 enters Cheddar from the west on 28th May 1960. The goods shed (behind the engine) still stands. PHOTOGRAPH R.E. TOOP.

grown in proliferation on the south-facing slopes of the hills, particularly around Draycott. The line had intermediate stations at Congresbury (1m 46ch from Yatton), Sandford (later renamed Sandford & Banwell - 4m 40ch), Woodborough (5m 55ch), Axbridge (8m 1ch), Cheddar (9m 64ch), Draycott (11m 70ch) and Lodge Hill (14m 2ch). A station was added at Wookey (16m 37ch) in 1871.

At Woodborough, the station nameboard, if legend is to be believed, originally presented problems. The locals commented on the use of hieroglyphics, but its odd appearance was due to the fact that the chap who had erected it could not read and, unknowingly, had fixed it upside down. In its 'correct' position, the nameboard hardly had time to settle on its mountings as, in December 1869, the station was renamed Winscombe. The renaming was to avoid confusion among the nation's ticket office staff, as the GWR already had a station named Woodborough, on the line between Savernake and Westbury in neighbouring Wiltshire.

The original buildings at Woodborough (alias Winscombe) station were constructed from timber, but in 1905 were replaced by buildings of Mendip limestone. Wookey station also had timber platform buildings (retained until the end) but the other stations on the line had stone buildings which were typical of many mid-Victorian West Country branches.

The most important of the intermediate stations was at Cheddar. Befitting the status of the community it served, it was the main crossing place on the line and, consequently, had two platforms. The only other intermediate twin-platform station on the line was at Axbridge which, incidentally, retained its original 13-lever B&ER signal box on the down platform until July 1907. All the intermediate stations had goods facilities, and several later acquired private sidings.

some 'connections' at the B&ER and the ESR stations left all of one minute for passengers to sprint from one station to the other although, in practice, the trains were usually held until the last of the breathless passengers had made it. The timings were, however, officially revised before too long.

The B&ER station was usually referred to as Tucker Street but, although that designation appeared in *Bradshaw's* at a fairly early stage, it was not formally adopted until July 1920. The suffix was dispensed with in May 1950, despite the fact that the old SCR station at Priory Road was still operational. Any possible confusion was, however, short-lived, as Priory Road station was closed to passengers on 29th October 1951.

The Yatton - Wells section became known as the 'Strawberry Line' on account of the little red delicacies which, avian depredations permitting, were

On 28th May 1960 2-6-2T No.41240 pauses at Cheddar before continuing to Yatton. PHOTOGRAPH R.E. TOOP.

Crossing at Axbridge - No.41240 pulls into the station with a train for Wells, while No.82035 waits to depart for Yatton. PHOTOGRAPH R.E. TOOP.

A pannier tank at a quiet rural station - what could be more redolent of the GWR and all its works? The engine is No.3731 at Cheddar, facing Witham, on 24th August 1956. PHOTOGRAPH R.M. CASSERLEY.

Over the years, some of the other stations were subjected to alterations. Sandford had a crossing loop (for goods trains only) installed in December 1905, the original signalbox being replaced by a new 31-lever box at the same time. Winscombe and Wookey were each treated to a platform extension around 1900, while the down platform at Axbridge was extended (to 340ft) in April 1909.

At Wells, the B&ER's exclusion from the East Somerset premises necessitated the provision of its own goods facilities and a separate engine shed. The goods shed was just to the north of the station - on the other side of the bridge under Tucker Street - while a

single-road engine shed and 44ft turntable were installed beyond the terminus end of the station. The enforced self-sufficiency of the three independent railway companies in Wells resulted in England's smallest city having three stations, three goods depots, and three engine sheds. That remarkable situation prevailed until the late 1870s.

For the citizens of Wells the B&ER offered easy connections at Yatton for Bristol, whereas the ESR provided, at best, a circuitous route to Bath or, in the event of an emergency, Yeovil. Predictably, traffic figures on the ESR suffered. The company courted the Great Western with a view to absorption, and

in December 1872 named a purchase price of £86,680. The GWR was interested in buying, but not at that sum, and negotiations broke down the following June.

Eighteen months later - in January 1874 - the GWR informed the ESR that it intended to convert the Bath - Frome - Castle Cary - Weymouth line to the narrow (i.e.standard) gauge. It was, therefore, essential that the ESR be similarly converted, but the estimated cost of the work was £7,390. The struggling little company had no hope of coughing up such a sum, and although advised that the GWR might legally be responsible for the costs, the ESR didn't have the funds (or the stomach) to challenge the GWR in court.

The safest option was to reopen negotiations for selling out to the GWR. This time, of course, it was the GWR which could call the tune, and the price offered was £67,442. Inevitably, the beleaguered East Somerset accepted, and it was formally absorbed by the GWR in December 1874. Just over a year later - in January 1876 - the GWR took the B&ER into its fold.

The GWR Regime

Shortly after taking over the ESR, the GWR had (in conjunction with the B&ER) laid the much-discussed connection between Tucker Street station and the ex-ESR station. The new arrangements were inspected by Colonel Yolland in April 1875:

'An Exchange Platform has been constructed in the East Somerset Station yard for passengers to change carriages, who may be proceeding in the narrow gauge trains of the Great West-

41249 pulls away from Tucker Street with the 2.52pm (SO) Wells - Yatton train on 23rd April 1960. The road bridge survives at the time of writing (April 1995) though possibly not for much longer. PHOTOGRAPH HUGH BALLANTYNE.

WELLS TUCKER STREET

Year	Staff		Passenger Traffic			Goods Traffic									livet'k (vans)	Total rec. £
	Total	Wages £	Tickets		Receipts total £	Forwarded (tons)			Received (tons)			coal not charged (tons)	goods total			
			issued	season		coal	mins.	gen.	coal	mins.	gen.		tons	rec. £		
1903	23	1540	53745	?	7650	-	438	1415	4354	534	5145	822	12708	5525	386	13175
1913	22	1827	45175	?	7312	59	1897	1587	2844	2183	3987	1024	13581	6089	190	13401
1923	23	3797	34167	49	10993	-	15824	1351	3081	1241	7302	428	29227	16820	249	27813
1924	23	3631	33453	39	10955	-	65868	1292	3115	2606	7807	486	81174	30588	286	41543
1925	22	3731	32321	22	8912	22	83549	1135	3782	2330	8119	1414	100351	36042	311	44954
1926	23	3753	26777	18	8091	51	68059	1521	3100	2397	8154	2468	85750	33013	243	41104
1927	23	3723	26678	18	8082	31	78766	1524	3345	2087	7854	2077	95684	39186	212	47268
1928	23	3792	23427	11	8255	33	53312	1865	2580	2347	8155	2675	70967	31662	232	39917
1929	23	3757	19774	26	7518	49	39108	1788	2965	1942	8366	2526	56744	25244	246	32762
1930	20	3535	14690	22	6057	10	34100	1699	3083	1214	8510	2208	50824	25059	218	31116
1931	20	3256	10976	31	5286	7	40892	2236	2706	929	7677	1752	66199	27296	177	32582
1932	19	3216	10390	25	4900	-	12931	1670	2484	949	7948	1467	27449	15382	111	20282
1933	19	3068	10977	44	4897	40	62013	2342	1840	1853	6984	1602	76674	37560	112	42457

ern Railway eastwards or in the broad gauge carriages of the Bristol & Exeter Railway westwards along the Cheddar Valley Railway. Provision is made for the Engines of the Great Western Railway to run round their trains after arriving at their Wells station from the east, by means of a mixed gauge loop line lying south of the Bristol & Exeter passenger line and which is also used by the engines of the latter company.

'From the position of the points etc., the Great Western engines cannot get from the western to the eastern end of their trains without first closing the Level Crossing gates, partly crossing the turnpike road [at the eastern end of the S&D station] and then shunting back along the loop line; and it is quite possible that hereafter complaints may be made on this subject by the road authorities.

'The arrangements thus carried out comply with the requirements of the Board of Trade, and great pains have been taken to make such arrangements of the sidings, points and their connection with the signals by interlocking etc., as to provide against the danger inherent in crossing so many goods lines on the level, but it must be distinctly understood that these arrangements are not suitable for working the passenger trains through Wells as a through station.

No.82009 reaches the summit of the 1 in 75 climb west of Cranmore on 23rd April 1960. The second carriage of the 3.28pm Witham - Yatton train appears to be a chocolate and cream slip coach. PHOTOGRAPH HUGH BALLANTYNE.

The 2.45pm Yatton - Witham, with No.41202 in charge, climbs from Shepton Mallet towards Cranmore on 23rd April 1960. PHOTOGRAPH HUGH BALLANTYNE.

CRANMORE															
Year	Staff		Passenger Traffic			Goods Traffic								livest'k (vans)	Total rec. £
	Total	Wages £	Tickets		Receipts total £	Forwarded (tons)			Received (tons)			coal not charged (tons)	goods total		
			issued	season		coal	mins.	gen.	coal	mins.	gen.		tons	rec. £	
1903	5	262	6323	?	1911	-	72655	367	1000	659	1138	121	76940	13489	85	15400
1913	5	319	6260	?	1228	-	69800	936	619	517	1597	479	73948	12899	60	14127
1923	6	945	6845	6	1719	-	63960	450	1290	832	1761	284	68557	23686	60	25405
1924	6	890	6536	10	973	-	79525	369	1245	1029	2503	193	84864	30626	57	31599
1925	6	880	5903	9	1058	-	110829	423	935	1034	2109	740	116070	42183	51	43241
1926	6	880	4974	16	971	-	111269	307	535	1041	2593	670	116415	42737	45	43708
1927	6	952	5550	25	1183	9	113282	471	904	1242	2773	724	119396	46742	23	47925
1928	7	1018	5127	18	1199	-	103459	447	760	1378	1415	780	108248	42281	34	43480
1929	7	1035	4571	71	1015	-	110299	663	562	1510	1079	1449	115562	46145	18	47160
1930	7	1068	3904	82	901	-	105294	527	436	1362	858	1359	109836	44232	18	45133
1931	7	1054	3771	78	1090	-	123921	362	396	1207	747	1189	127822	48639	24	49729
1932	7	1062	2669	83	706	-	128101	303	338	1353	620	665	131380	48257	3	48963
1933	6	1004	2687	89	485	11	108987	211	248	1407	563	633	112060	37292	13	37777

'I should however state that the pillars which support the roof that covers the Exchange Platform in the East Somerset Station yard are placed at a distance of about 4ft 8in to 5 feet of the south edge of this platform, the requirement of the Board of Trade being 6 feet.

'This may be recognised as a mere temporary arrangement, on receipt of an undertaking from the

Cranmore station in pre-preservation days - the date is 21st August 1958 and the train is the 3.28pm Witham - Yatton. PHOTOGRAPH HUGH BALLANTYNE.

4th May 1963, and No.41248 pulls away from the small but well-maintained station at Wookey, with the 2pm Yatton - Wells. PHOTOGRAPH MICHAEL MENSING.

Great Western Company to alter the position of these pillars and to give the required width in the course of six months; but in the absence of any such undertaking, I must report that this single line cannot be opened for passenger traffic without danger to the public. I must not, moreover, be understood to assent to the present construction of this Station so far as it renders it necessary to shunt engines etc., across the turnpike road.

'A good deal has been done by the Bristol & Exeter Company in carrying out these works to render the working into and out of the Somerset & Dorset Passenger Station safe, but there are still sidings lying south of their passenger lines which are not provided with blind sidings to throw off points to prevent vehicles from being brought out of them without the sanction of the Signalman on duty'.

In other words, permission to oper-

ate passenger trains via the new connection was refused.

The ESR line from Witham had been converted to the standard gauge in June 1874, but the former Bristol & Exeter line from Yatton was not converted until November 1875. The mixed gauge rails on the S&D line into Wells had, incidentally, remained in use until 1868, a broad gauge B&ER goods train having operated daily from Bristol to Wells via Highbridge.

The conversion of the Yatton - Wells line was not inspected for the Board of Trade until September 1876, the Inspecting Officer finding that a rail had simply been moved on the sleepers, leaving them two feet longer at one end than at the other.(!) The Board of Trade, with a shake, almost, of its institutional head, 'recommended' that the rails should be put in the middle of the sleepers, and the extra two feet cut off. The fishplates, moreover, fitted imperfectly and the bolts in many cases did not come through the rails. 'Better arrangements' (the tone almost approaches that used to a small and precocious child) were ordered 'to prevent needless multiplication of cases where rails of different sections meet'. There was an even more bizarre aspect to all this - absurdly, three miles were laid on a gauge *a quarter of an inch narrower* than the standard narrow gauge, a situation that had come abut somewhat mysteriously, 'under the verbal orders of Mr John Fox, who was the resident Engineer...'

The report certainly suggests a somewhat unsafe stretch of railway, but it had been in regular use for ten months, apparently without mishaps...

After the gauge conversion, the arrangements at Wells seemed to attract considerable attention from the GWR hierarchy. On 2nd November 1876 the

The 3pm Wells - Yatton train has just passed Wookey without stopping. The engine is No.41248 and the date 4th May 1963. PHOTOGRAPH MICHAEL MENSING.

The 2.45pm Yatton - Witham train, hauled by 2-6-2T No.82039, crosses the S&D line after leaving Shepton Mallet on 4th May 1963. The Mendip Hills lie in the distance. PHOTOGRAPH MICHAEL MENSING.

company's Deputy Chairman, Alexander Wood, visited Wells, and subsequently reported that:

'The first thing which attracted my attention [at the old ESR station] was a new First Class Coach, sent from Swindon upon the order of Mr.Stephenson. I subsequently learned that, at Wells, there was no advice of this vehicle's arrival, and that being destined to relieve a B&E coach it had been sent to the wrong Station at Wells; and to reach the right one [in a revenue-earning capacity] it had to go via Bristol! I merely mention this as a forcible illustration of the very great importance of connecting our two Wells Stations at the earliest moment.

'The next thing in the Station yard that attracted my attention was the Cattle Pens. They evidently have been disused for sometime. As much as four months previously the Government Inspector, in consequence of the pens not being paved, had condemned them and prohibited their use.

'The only cattle now passing to or from the Great Western Railway system at Wells station, on the Witham branch, is loaded or unloaded at the Passenger Station and on the Passenger Platform. It certainly seemed to me to be a most objectionable arrangement.

'As regards the general goods, the South Western and Midland goods were delivered regularly between 9 and 10am, but ours remain undelivered until between 2 and 3pm.

'As regards the passenger traffic, our best train [from Wells to London] is the 1.10, timed to run in 4 hours and 40 minutes. By our morning train run from Swindon at express fares, passengers are on the road upwards of five hours, while if they do not pay express fares from Swindon, upwards of six hours. The South Western convey their passengers from Wells to London, starting at a more convenient time than ours, accomplishing the journey without express fares, and in very little over 4 hours'.

GWR crossing the S&D - the 3.28pm Witham - Yatton train approaches Shepton Mallet on 4th May 1963. Engine is No.41249. PHOTOGRAPH MICHAEL MENSING.

On 4th May 1963, No.41249 descends towards Shepton Mallet with the 3.28pm Witham - Yatton train. PHOTOGRAPH MICHAEL MENSING.

Having just passed Dulcote Quarry (to the east of Wells), No.82039 continues with the 6.20pm Witham - Wells train on 4th May 1963. PHOTOGRAPH MICHAEL MENSING.

SHEPTON MALLET															
Year	Staff		Passenger Traffic			Goods Traffic								livest'k (vans)	Total reo. £
	Total	Wages £	Tickets		Receipts total £	Forwarded (tons)			Received (tons)			coal not charged (tons)	goods total		
			issued	season		ooal	mins.	gen.	ooal	mins.	gen.		tons	reo. £	
1903	15	814	29631	?	3998	-	993	16580	9378	545	12634	450	40580	18905	265	22903
1913	16	942	25010	?	3283	30	638	15121	9273	697	11777	1156	38692	19229	625	22512
1923	13	1690	18584	35	4130	38	45	835	2778	384	6682	2012	12774	8930	440	13060
1924	13	1656	16423	29	3968	9	155	724	3241	807	5930	2159	13025	8526	531	12494
1925	12	1690	16227	30	4207	8	206	755	2601	449	6346	2105	12470	8974	584	13181
1926	12	1678	11100	25	3606	19	159	707	1554	583	5929	2445	11396	8350	547	11956
1927	12	1748	11436	21	3927	15	51	754	1948	1155	6247	2873	13043	9786	676	13713
1928	12	1647	10141	39	3983	50	125	675	1811	962	5037	2394	11054	8442	523	12425
1929	12	1682	9424	65	3548	8	172	677	2024	618	4745	2225	10469	8035	498	11583
1930	11	1630	8093	82	3350	-	-	652	1762	253	4645	929	8241	7475	470	10825
1931	11	1510	7289	94	2811	-	-	426	1260	695	4125	953	7550	7158	448	9969
1932	10	1444	6320	85	2530	-	-	354	1281	850	2961	1019	6465	5509	397	8039
1933	10	1376	6308	88	2465	-	88	462	1536	173	2897	908	6064	5205	271	7670

0-6-0 No.2268 approaches Dulcote Quarry with the 6.15pm Yatton - Witham on 4th May 1963. PHOTOGRAPH MICHAEL MENSING.

Mr Wood was clearly displeased. One of those who came under attack was the GWR's Chief Goods Manager, John Grant, who promptly replied on the subject of the goods traffic: 'The late delivery of the London traffic at Wells has for some time past been complained of, and although there is now some improvement I am not satisfied that it will continue.

'The London traffic for Wells is conveyed by the 11.35pm train which is due at Witham at 8am. The Witham branch goods train leaves at 8.35, and if the London train keeps proper time the goods would be at Wells at 9.20am. The London train is, however, frequently late, so that the branch train has had to leave without the London goods, which are then detained at Witham until the 12 noon which reaches Wells at 12.40pm.

'Formerly the Weymouth train which conveys the Wells traffic to Witham started at 11.15am and reached Witham about half an hour earlier than at present, but the time of this train had to be altered and put later in order that a new and important narrow gauge train from Swindon to Exeter should start at 11.15am'.

In January 1877, a report (nominally written by the GWR's General Manager, James Grierson) on the working of Wells station was presented. The delay in improving the crossing arrangements (to the satisfaction of the BoT) at Wells was summarily excused by the pressure of work on the company's engineering staff, but the report devoted a little more space to other matters: 'With regard to the GWR cattle pens having been closed by the Cattle Inspector ....an estimate was submitted for paving the pens, but it was considered undesirable to recommend the Board incur the expenditure, estimated at £44.4s.6d.

'From the memorandum of the Deputy Chairman, he seemed to be under the impression (1) that the cattle trade of Wells is a large trade and (2) that this Company lost a considerable proportion of it because the pens were closed'.

Receipts for three years (1874, 1875 and 1876) were given: for Wells GWR the sums were £448, £500 and £474, and for Wells B&E £185, £202 and £345 respectively. 'From those figures' Grierson concluded with a flourish, the cattle business at Wells was, demonstrably, ' a very small traffic'.

With regard to a service of trains between Yatton and Witham, Grierson considered it 'manifest' that the working could not be improved - 'owing to the difficulty of meeting the through

In this undated picture, 0-4-2T No.1465 leaves Yatton with a train for Wells. Yatton West box can be seen behind the rear carriage. The engine's number has been confirmed with the aid of a powerful magnifying glass, and so a mystery arises. It had been renumbered (from 4865) in November 1946, and spent all but four months of its subsequent life in the Oswestry District (often at Machynlleth, sometimes at Penmaenpool or Aberayron). The outstanding period of four months is accounted for by six weeks at Stafford Road factory for a heavy general (8/12/49 to 20/1/50), almost five weeks at Stafford Road for a heavy intermediate (25/11/53 to 30/12/53), and a month or so at Slough (from 4/10/56). So how came it to be sporting a late-1940s/early-1950s livery on a Yatton - Wells working?

route continued to be regarded as separate entities and, even by the mid-1880s, only four trains worked right through each weekday. For the record, they were the 11.45am passenger from Yatton (arr. Witham 1.40pm), a goods from Bristol via Yatton, and two goods workings from Witham (via Wells and Yatton) to Bristol. Working timetables (WTTs) for the mid-1880s, incidentally, include an early morning goods train from Yatton which had a passenger carriage (or carriages) attached at Cheddar, thereby completing the journey to Wells as a mixed train.

The rationalisation of workings in Wells resulted in the closure of the ex-B&ER engine shed, its locomotives being transferred to the old ESR shed. Some sources indicate that the ex-B&ER shed was actually closed in 1876, which is quite feasible; not only had the GWR take-over of the B&ER resulted in the former having two engine sheds at Wells, but the connecting line between Tucker Street and the ESR station was then in position, and could legally have been used for light engine movements.

Whatever the case, the old ESR shed didn't have very long to bask in its new-found glory as, in September 1879, it was demolished to make way for a new 75ft-long twin-road shed on the same site. This had a 40ft turntable which, presumably, came from the old ESR shed. The 'table at Tucker Street remained *in situ* until the late 1920s, a GWR Locomotive Committee minute of 31st March 1927 authorising £480 to be spent on: 'Removal of the turntable near the [GWR] engine shed and the transfer of the turntable from Tucker Street in replacement'.

After the alterations to the arrangements at Wells, the Yatton - Witham branch settled down to a steady existence. The air of routine was, however, shattered on 8th May 1889 by an accident on the Wells - Witham section. The contemporary description gives a good insight into engines and stock of

trains at Witham and Yatton by running the engines and trains through between those stations, there not being sufficient traffic to justify the running of increased mileage'. The great difficulty in working the branch was the fourteen miles of single line without a crossing place. Grierson gave instructions to see what the cost would be of providing passing places at Cranmore and Shepton Mallet and plans were accordingly prepared. To no great surprise, the cost was deemed to be 'so very great'. Grierson *desired the Engineer to devise some more economical method of providing means for passing two trains, and it was agreed to give up the idea at present of a crossing place at Shepton Mallet and only to construct one at Cranmore'.* The sub-

ject of a crossing place at Cranmore remained under consideration, though the first crossing place to be installed was, in fact, at Shepton - in 1895. Cranmore did not receive similar treatment until 1904. At both stations, second platforms were added.

The problems of the connecting line between the two stations at Wells were eventually resolved, and from 1 January 1878 trains between Witham and Wells ran the extra few hundred yards to and from Tucker Street station. The former-ESR station was closed to passengers, and subsequently became the city's main goods depot.

The new arrangements at Wells did not, however, result in *all* branch services operating through between Yatton and Witham. The two sections of the

A quite perfect view of Tucker Street station at Wells - No.82040 pulls away with a Yatton - Witham train on 16th June 1962. **PHOTOGRAPH MICHAEL J. FOX.**

Yatton shed, 25th May 1953. The building stood almost alongside the start of the Clevedon branch, on the north side of the station. PHOTOGRAPH R.C. RILEY.

the time - several coaches of the 9.40am train from Wells had left the rails when the train was in the Studley cutting, about a mile and a half south of Witham, but nobody was hurt. The passenger train consisted of a six-wheel coupled tank engine, running chimney first, and five four-wheel coaches, the first and last being 'brake-vans'. The guard was travelling in the last coach, 'and could work Fay's brake on all the coaches'. The train was travelling at a speed of about 25 to 30 miles an hour. It got over safely, but the brake-coach was a light vehicle and seems to have been jerked off the rails and to have become uncoupled from the engine about this time.

In his report, Colonel Rich pointed out that three new longitudinal sleepers and five new transoms had been put into the permanent way two days before the accident, and concluded that the derailment had been caused by the track not having been properly packed under the sleepers when the work had been undertaken. In his summing-up, Col. Rich opined that: *'Fay's brake did good service, and if the train had been fitted with a good automatic continuous brake, under the control of the engine driver as well as of the guard, it is probable that no damage would have been done'.*

The Yatton - Witham branch grew an appendage on 4th December 1901

when the Wrington Vale Light Railway opened to the public. The WVLR had been authorised under the terms of the Light Railways Act of 1896, but had been constructed by the GWR. It took the form of a six and a half mile branch between Congresbury and Blagdon, with intermediate stations at Wrington, Langford and Burrington. It was not anticipated that this Blagdon branch would be intensively used but the 'junction' station at Congresbury nevertheless had a second platform added (the loop was brought into use on 14th April 1901) and was necessarily resignalled, a new 43-lever box opening at the station at the same time, to replace the 8-lever box of 1876.

One of the less well-photographed stations on the Cheddar Valley line - Draycott. No.82009 enters with a Yatton train on 21st March 1960. PHOTOGRAPH E.T. GILL.

Lest it be thought that the Wells branch was all pretty country trains, this view clearly shows the other face of things - Merehead Quarry, near Cranmore. The A361 Shepton Mallet - Frome road cuts across the lower edge of the picture, the Wells - Witham railway line being a little out of view behind the photographer (pilot?). This picture was taken soon after the opening of the new spur into the quarry, in August 1970.

The usual practice was for Blagdon trains to run through to or from Yatton, but some (especially on peak season Saturdays in the 1920s) started and terminated at Congresbury to avoid adding to the congestion at Yatton. The potential problem of Blagdon trains adding to the peak-time melee at Yatton was, however, not long-lived, passenger services being withdrawn from the Blagdon branch on 14th September 1931. Sadly, the story of the WVLR is beyond the remit of this modest article. A short but interesting history of the line can, however, be found in *The Wrington Vale Light Railway* (Avon-Anglia 1978).

In the early part of the 1900s, it seemed that the Wells - Shepton Mallet section of the Yatton - Witham branch might be the subject of a minor power struggle involving the Somerset & Dorset Railway which, by then, was operated by a joint committee. In the event, battle did not even commence. The conclusion of the matter was concisely summed up in an S&D Traffic Committee minute of 4th May 1910: *'With reference to the suggestion put forward by the Wells Corporation and other Local Authorities in the district that the Joint Committee should obtain running powers over the Great Western Railway between Wells and Shepton Mallet and construct a junction loop at the latter place for a direct through service to Bath and the North, it was agreed that the proposal be not entertained'.*

Perhaps ironically, from 1st October 1934 - over four years after an administrative review had effectively put at an end the S&D's corporate existence - GWR trains called at the ex-S&D station (Priory Road) in Wells en route to and from Witham. The practice continued until the closure of Priory Road station in October 1951.

Trains and Traffic

On the Yatton - Witham branch, the weekday passenger services listed in the WTT for the summer of 1910 comprised four each way between Yatton and Witham (one of which ran as a 'mixed' from Wells to Witham) three each way between Yatton and Wells, two each way between Wells and Witham, and one each way between Yatton and Shepton Mallet. There were also five Blagdon branch trains in each direction on the Yatton - Congresbury section.

The 1910 WTT showed that the majority of the passenger workings on the Yatton - Witham line ran through to or from Bristol or, in some cases, Bath or Frome (usually via Radstock). Indeed, a circular Bristol - Radstock - Frome - Witham - Wells - Yatton - Bristol tour was a regular feature of the WTTs for many years. Other services listed in the 1910 WTT originated a little farther afield, the 11.58am ex-Yatton to Shepton Mallet and its return working (1.50pm ex-Shepton), and the 7.15pm ex-Yatton to Wells (no return working) all being marked as 'Severn Tunnel Passenger'. The corresponding public timetable is not to hand - maybe it was that the stock worked to and from Severn Tunnel Junction, but was not regarded as a through service. If appropriate, polite correction would be welcome.

By the summer of 1922, the public timetables listed four trains each way between Yatton and Cheddar on weekdays, two between Yatton and Wells, one between Yatton and Cheddar, and one (listed as a motor train) between Wells and Witham. As with the 1910 timetables, there was one Yatton - Witham passenger train each way on Sundays.

As already mentioned, the Yatton - Witham line was not solely dependent on its revenue from passengers. Far from it. For centuries, the local population had seemed hell-bent on digging things up - firstly it was Fullers Earth, then it was coal, and when the collieries started to close, attention turned to stone. North Somerset is not usually thought of as being in any way industrial, but quarrying is still big business in the area, to this day.

Year	1947	1076 0-6-0ST/PT	1854 0-6-0PT	Dean Goods 0-6-0	388 0-6-0	4500 2-6-2T	2251 0-6-0	5800 0-4-2T	5700 0-6-0PT
1923		1574, 1604		2384					
1924	1456, 1492	1626, 1646							
1925	1453, 1492, 1499	1574	1752	2422	1188				
1926		1619, 1624		2330		4572			
1927	1463	1619, 1624		2451		4572			
1928	1463	1619, 1624		2338		4572			
1929		1624		2398		5557			
1930		1624, 1565				4596, 5536			
1931				2473		4507, 5557			
1932						5549	2260		
1933						4585			
1934				2400		5564			
1935				2567					
1936						4595	2260		
1937				2573		5561			
1938						5536	2252	5801	
1939						5514, 5540			
1940						4580	2293		
1941				2563		5557			
1942				2445			2258		
1943						4577	2220		
1944						5553, 5557	2258		
1945							2253		
1946						5572	2220		
1947						4595	2253		4619
1948						5506	2258		

Locomotives at Wells shed, 1923-1948. Allocations are for first week of January each year.

4056 PRINCESS MARGARET comes into Yatton on 25th May 1953, a scene long prepared for the Coronation that year. PHOTOGRAPH R.C. RILEY.

From the mid-1920s - when various siding connections to quarries between Wells and Witham were installed or improved - stone provided an increasing amount of traffic for the branch. The peak years were 1926, 1927 and 1928, when over 300,000 tons of stone were exported annually by rail. At the time, that represented around three quarters of the branch's total goods traffic. To put a different perspective on the relationship between passenger and mineral traffic, from 1924 the passenger traffic accounted for just a third (or less) of the line's total income.

Towards the western end of the Yatton - Wells line, a standard gauge siding to Sandford Quarry (for Messrs. J.Aird) was laid in 1903, with an internal narrow gauge system in the quarry itself. The narrow gauge finally closed around 1940, but the standard gauge siding (latterly serving Messrs. Roads Reconstruction and worked by a 4-wheel Sentinel) was not taken out of use until September 1964. One of Sandford Quarry's main products, incidentally, was ballast.

At Cheddar, sidings for the Callow Rock Lime Co. were installed in September 1922, for Messrs. Butcher & Ford (Batts Coombe Quarry Co) in July 1926, and for Messrs. L.W. Bryant in October 1935. The last-named had, however, gone out of business by October 1936. Wookey had a little more variety in the way of such traffic, a siding being laid to the Mendip Paper Mill (later St.Cuthbert's Paper Works) by March 1880 and another for the benefit of the Somerset County Council quarry in March 1920. The paper works siding at Wookey lasted - nominally, at least - until June 1965, but the quarry siding had been taken out of use in July 1948 and removed in 1950.

The biggest quarries were to the east of Wells. The first to have a connection to the Wells - Witham line was Waterlip Quarry, near Cranmore, where a horse-worked tramway was opened circa 1871. A standard gauge locomotive-worked extension was laid to Downhead Quarry about 1907. Downhead ceased operating in the mid-1920s, but activities at Waterlip continued until 1946. At its peak, Waterlip Quarry had produced enough stone for a hundred wagons each day. Near Waterlip quarry, Messrs. Roads Reconstruction (later part of the ARC group) established a plant depot which serviced the numerous standard and narrow gauge quarry engines of north east Somerset.

Three other quarries in the immediate area - at Doulting, Dulcote and Merehead - had their own internal narrow gauge railway systems, although that at Doulting was horse-worked. At Dulcote, the siding connection to the quarry was altered in 1923, worked from a ground frame locked by key on the electric train staff. There was a very steeply falling gradient for the greater part of the distance between Shepton Mallet and Wells, and special instructions were printed and issued in regard to the working of these sidings, involving not only the prohibition of any vehicles being left on the main line when shunting operations were going on but also the setting of the new siding connection as a trap before movements on to the single line could be allowed over the old connection. A new siding arrangement had also been instituted between Wookey and Wells, in 1920, and the usefulness of the new facilities may be gauged from the quantities of stone booked from the two stations - some 100,000 tons or more by the mid-1920s.

The local strawberry trade provided some business for the railway but, of course, it was highly seasonal. That said, almost until the demise of the branch in the 1960s, special trains were run from Cheddar and Draycott during the picking season to transport the produce of over 250 holdings. Standard bogie goods vans and, during the 1950s, Siphon Gs (marked 'Return to Yatton') were stabled at Cheddar all year round in readiness for their brief burst of seasonal activity. The strawberry business had, at one time, also given an indirect boost to the railway. In Victorian and Edwardian days, many town and city dwellers had found that they could afford summer holidays only by combining it with work as pickers, and some managed to travel by rail. It was the Somerset equivalent of hop-picking holidays in Kent, albeit on a far smaller scale.

The last WTT issued by the GWR (6th October 1947 to 30th May 1948 - admittedly a winter season WTT) listed three weekday passenger services from Yatton to Witham (the 7.25am Bristol - Frome and two diesel railcar workings) and five in the opposite direction (7.53am ex-Trowbridge to Bristol, 10.10am Frome - Bristol diesel, 10.17am ex-Bristol via Frome and Witham to Yatton, 3.27pm Frome - Bristol, and 5.20pm ex-Bristol via Frome). There were also five services from Yatton to Wells, but only three in the opposite direction, and one each way between Wells and Witham. There was one Yatton - Witham service each way on Sundays.

At Yatton, the Wells and Witham trains were nominally allocated a bay at the rear of the down platform. However, a proportion of branch workings originated or terminated at Bristol (as evidenced above) and so, for many years, the branch bay at Yatton was not always used. That said, it is worth noting that the public timetables for the winter of 1960/61 showed that six of the seven down trains to Wells each day originated at Yatton while four of the six up trains terminated there - the branch bay was clearly in more regular use by then. The bay's use by Blagdon (WVLR) services had, incidentally, ceased in 1931, that branch having lost its passenger services in September of that year.

The goods workings of the late 1940s included two each way between Yatton and Wells (one of the up trains heading for St.Philips Marsh, the others to/from West Depot), one from West Depot to Cheddar which returned to Stoke Gifford, and three each way (principally for stone traffic) on the Witham - Wells section. '2251' 0-6-0s (which worked many of the branch's goods services) were restricted to a 140-ton loading on the most steeply-graded sections east of Wells - many of the stone trains exceeded that weight, and so it was fairly common practice for trains hauled by '2251s' to be split into two, each part being taken up separately. The working instructions for the period reveal that through trains nominally changed direction at Wells. From Yatton, a train ran *down* as far as Wells, but was regarded as an up working from there to Witham. This is a clear indication that the branch was, even then, regarded as two separate lines - that is, Yatton - Wells and Wells - Witham. The instructions also explain that the branch was worked by electric train staff between Cheddar and Wells, but electric train *token* on the Yatton - Cheddar and Wells - Witham sections. The intermediate crossing places at Sandford, Lodge Hill, Wookey and Wells (ESR Yard) were approved for two freight trains crossing, or a freight and a passenger, but were on no account to be used for two passenger trains to cross.

By the summer of 1955, the public timetables listed a healthy number of services on the branch. On weekdays, there were three each way between Yatton and Witham (an extra Witham - Yatton service being provided on Saturdays) four each way between Yatton and Wells (plus an SX Wells to Yatton) two from Witham to Wells and one from Wells to Witham. It should, however, be emphasised that the above is only a summary - some of the timings varied enormously for the SX and SO services. The Sunday service of the period (summer timetables only) consisted of one Yatton - Wells and one Wells - Yatton train each way.

Motive Power

During broad gauge days 4-4-0STs had been the usual locomotives, but after gauge conversion various types of 0-6-0STs were used. Almost inevitably, the 'Metro' 2-4-0Ts eventually took over most of the passenger workings, but they were superseded in the mid-1920s by '4500' class 2-6-2Ts, which remained active on the branch until the late 1950s. It is believed that 'Bulldog' 4-4-0s were also occasionally used on the line until the 1930s.

Goods workings were usually handled by tank and tender 0-6-0s, the classic 'Dean Goods' maintaining a presence on the line until the 1940s. The '2251' 0-6-0s first appeared soon after their debut in 1930, and by the 1940s monopolised the goods turns. The useful Churchward 2-6-0s were not excluded from the branch, but to the best of my memory at least, they played second fiddle to the 0-6-0s.

From the late 1930s, the GWR diesel railcars (based at St.Philips Marsh shed in Bristol) appeared on the branch, and by the early 1950s SPM had two railcar diagrams which included duties on the line. One diagram took in the 10.10am Frome - Yatton service and the 2.47pm Yatton-Frome, the other including the 5.10pm (SX) Bristol Temple Meads - Wells (via Yatton) and the 7.00pm return from Wells.

The Yatton - Witham branch was nominally serviced by the sheds at Yatton and Wells, both of which were outstations of Bath Road in Bristol, but as some of the branch trains ran through to or from Bristol (or elsewhere), the role of the two sub-sheds was limited. Yatton's main purpose was to service the Clevedon branch,

one of a trio '1400' class 0-4-2Ts being outstationed at Yatton shed for a week at a time for Clevedon duties. A second Bath Road engine (until the mid-1950s, often a '5800' 0-4-2T) was outstationed at Yatton for use on shunting and pilot duties, plus the daily freight on the Blagdon branch (which was truncated at Wrington on 1 November 1950), and the occasional trip to Wells. During the mid-1950s, four sets of crew were based at Yatton.

New forms of motive power started to appear on the Yatton - Witham line in 1955. An Ivatt '2MT' 2-6-0 (allegedly No 46457) was noted on the branch in January and, in August, Ivatt 2-6-2T No 41202 (which had recently been transferred to Bath Road shed) was observed on the 2.15pm Bristol - Witham. In 1958, the dieselisation of the Cardiff Valleys services resulted in the displacement of many Standard '3MT' 2-6-2Ts, and fourteen of them were transferred to Bath Road during the year. One of the first two to arrive at Bristol, No 82003, made its debut on the Yatton - Wells run in April.

By the latter part of the 1950s workings on the branch were dominated by '2MTs', '3MTs' and '2251s', but the '4500' 2-6-2Ts and, inevitably, 0-6-0PTs, were certainly not absent. Although smaller engines were normally used, the route was categorised as 'Dotted Blue' and, therefore, larger engines were nominally permitted. Until the early 1950s, the working instructions for the branch referred to certain restrictions being applied to 'Saint' class 4-6-0s while, during the

In this lovely GWR-era picture, 2-6-2T No.5514 waits at Tucker Street with the 12.34pm Yatton - Witham. The date is 21st April 1934. PHOTOGRAPH H.C. CASSERLEY.

Year	CONGRESBURY			SANDFORD & BANWELL			WINSCOMBE			AXBRIDGE			CHEDDAR			DRAYCOTT		
	receipts total £	staff no.	staff wages £	receipts total £	staff no.	staff wages £	receipts total £	staff no.	staff wages £	receipts total £	staff no.	staff wages £	receipts total £	staff no.	staff wages £	receipts total £	staff no.	staff wages £
1903	2230	5	275	3890	3	176	3527	2	109	6800	8	345	10897	8	424	1996	2	114
1913	2595	5	322	3804	5	326	4333	3	184	5792	7	497	7429	7	489	2537	3	180
1923	5096	5	859	38810	7	1092	7211	4	593	6899	8	1154	17285	9	1380	5059	3	621
1924	5738	5	830	42675	7	1103	7336	4	600	6553	8	1139	20624	10	1291	4766	3	566
1925	5981	5	870	41708	7	1143	6931	4	594	6433	7	1128	23033	9	1462	3889	3	558
1926	4696	5	850	37183	7	1083	5868	4	588	6287	7	1091	21568	9	1383	4187	3	502
1927	5060	5	858	38223	7	1128	6550	4	569	7571	7	1120	28871	11	1802	4288	3	504
1928	4704	5	852	21140	7	1120	6281	4	554	6441	7	1079	25466	12	1848	4117	3	484
1929	4374	5	842	18545	7	1049	5312	4	553	5797	7	1075	29765	12	1915	3668	3	484
1930	4280	5	769	12436	6	1008	4617	3	529	5517	6	1029	24632	12	1953	2590	3	477
1931	3819	5	781	14935	6	904	4417	3	481	4964	6	936	22667	12	1752	1495	3	488
1932	2719	5	729	8053	6	910	4078	3	469	4434	6	890	27217	11	1615	1527	3	470
1933	1895	5	768	3609	5	819	3352	3	466	4008	5	798	38158	11	1785	1411	2	381

Witham - Bristol, hauled by 2-6-2T No 82007, at Shepton Mallet.

Yatton shed closed in August 1960. It had been rendered redundant by the introduction, on 8th August, of DMUs on the Clevedon branch. The services on the Wells branch remained steam-hauled, but were subsequently worked from Bristol. Those, of course, were not the only changes of the period - in 1962 it was announced that one third of the traffic on the Yatton - Witham line was accounted for by schoolchildren travelling between Wells and Shepton Mallet. It was also alleged that the branch was losing over £50,000 a year...

It was subsequently proposed to withdraw the passenger services between Yatton and Witham, to close Lodge Hill station to all traffic, and to retain the facilities at Congresbury and Winscombe solely to deal with coal wagons. The review nevertheless recommended the retention of facilities at Cranmore for bitumen traffic and at Draycott for the seasonal strawberries - two daily trains during the six-week season, one to Bristol, the other to Birmingham Moor Street - but the substitution of road transport for the third 'strawberry special' which conveyed the fruit for destinations in the North of England and Scotland.

The withdrawal of passenger services did not take effect until 7th September 1963. The last eastbound passenger train was hauled by 0-6-0 No 2268 and, probably, the final westbound was worked by No 3218 of Wells shed. Latterly employing three drivers and four firemen, it closed two months

1950s, various restrictions were listed for BR Standard 'Class 4' and 'Manor' 4-6-0s. None of these 4-6-0s ever seem to have traversed the branch..

Changes Afoot

In 1958 the passenger services on the branch were revised, and this resulted in a complete lack of Wells - Yatton

elling to Clevedon and back behind 2-6-2T No 41249 (the usual engine, 0-4-2T No 1426, being serviced), left Yatton aboard the 2.52pm to Witham, hauled once again by No 41249. At Wells, 2-6-0 No 46525 was on goods duties while 2-6-2T No 41240 and 0-6-0PT No 3735 were also present. Continuing the journey, train crossed the 3.24pm

Looking from the west, Wanstrow station seemed rather more substantial than it actually was. 2-6-2T No.5540 approaches with the 10.10am Witham - Yatton train on 2nd July 1955. PHOTOGRAPH R.C. RILEY.

trains between 10.30am and 4.20pm. Sunday services were withdrawn completely. The timetable revision also resulted in the reduction of daily freight workings on the branch to just three. The first was timed to leave Bristol West Depot at 3.50am, arrive at Wells (ESR) at 6.59am, and leave for Bristol at 10.22am (9.45am on Saturdays). The second left West Depot at 9.30am, arrived at Wells at 2.50pm and returned at 4.40pm. The third was a pick-up working from Westbury, which entered the branch at Witham and terminated at Wells. The stone traffic from the various quarries along the branch was usually taken to Bristol for marshalling prior to distribution to other parts of the country.

Mr Eric Youldon made a precise record of a trip made on the line on Friday 29th July 1960 - a picture of operations is provided in the following notes: *2-6-0 No 46517 and 0-4-2T No 1426 were on shed at Yatton. After trav-*

With the western end of the Mendip Hills as backdrop, 0-6-0PT No.4647 pulls into Axbridge on 8th July 1959. PHOTOGRAPH H.C. CASSERLEY.

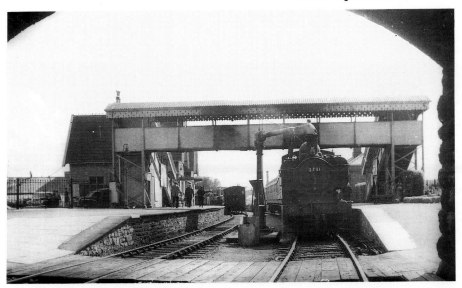

Wells Tucker Street - No.3731, framed in the bridge, waits with a Witham train on 24th August 1956. PHOTOGRAPH R.M. CASSERLEY.

Congresbury was the first station along the Cheddar Valley line from Yatton. This view, dated 8th July 1959, looks east, and was presumably taken from the now-removed bridge which carried the A370 road over the railway. PHOTOGRAPH R.M. CASSERLEY.

later. The little shed's survival had been due partly to the stone traffic which originated east of Wells and partly to the practice of regarding the Yatton - Wells and Wells - Witham sections as two separate entities.

Public goods facilities were retained at most of the branch stations only until 13 July 1964, but the Witham-Cheddar section clung on (albeit with the status of a siding) until 28 March

1969. By then, steam traction was a thing of the past. During the last year or so of passenger services on the line, North British 'Type 2' diesel-hydraulics had sometimes been used, while between 1965 and 1969 the goods workings were usually entrusted to 'Hymeks'. In the goods-only days, a Westbury-Cheddar pick-up goods operated each weekday, an additional train working as far as Cranmore on

Tuesdays, Thursdays and Saturdays.

In 1969 the branch was truncated at Dulcote. At the time, plans were afoot to develop Dulcote as a stone terminal while, a little to the east, the bitumen depot at Cranmore and the quarry at Merehead both continued to generate regular traffic. A new siding had, incidentally, been laid to Merehead in 1948. Cranmore's bitumen traffic ceased in September 1985 but, by then, the remains of the old East Somerset Railway had taken on an new and impressive significance.

The plans for the development of Dulcote were, however, abandoned in favour of nearby Merehead Quarry, and a new threequarter mile line into Merehead was opened in August 1970. In 1986 the quarry's owners, Messrs. Foster Yeoman, introduced their massive American-built 'Class 59' diesels - the first privately-owned locos to haul freight on BR's main lines.

It was not only the Merehead terminal which attracted attention. At Cranmore, the loss of the bitumen traffic did not spell the end of that station's life. In 1977 - eight years before the last bitumen train ran - David Shepherd's preservation organisation had started work on restoring the station and its yard as a base for operations. The title adopted was the East Somerset Railway, the same as that of the company which had opened the line through Cranmore in 1858. At first, the preservationists were restricted to a short stretch of line but, in 1985, they extended to a purpose-built halt called Mendip Vale.

The preserved line is, of course, still connected to the outside world at Witham, although ESR trains cannot normally operate east of Cranmore. Trains have, however, worked *into* Cranmore from Witham in the last few years - an HST special was run in 1990 and, in the spring of 1991, a Class 47 arrived at Cranmore with a train of nine Pullman sleeping cars. The Pullman's twenty passengers were Americans who had paid the sum of £3,000 each for a railtour of Britain. The 'Mendipman' railtour of 8th October 1994 worked through from Paddington to Cranmore and return, hauled by preserved No 5029 NUNNEY CASTLE.

As a final word on this sadly-missed branch line, much of the abandoned section west of Cranmore is still easily discernible today. Furthermore, most of the stations are substantially intact, several having been taken over for commercial use. At the ends of

| Year | LODGE HILL | | | WOOKEY | | | WELLS | | | SHEPTON MALLET | | | CRANMORE | | | WANSTROW | | |
| | receipts | staff | | receipts | staff | | receipts | staff | | receipts | staff | | receipts | staff | | receipts | staff | |
	total £	no.	wages £	total £	no.	wages £	total £	no.	wages £	total £	no.	wages £	total £	no.	wages £	total £	no.	wages £
1903	1927	2	120	8155	5	216	13175	23	1540	22903	15	814	15400	5	262	*	*	*
1913	2799	3	201	8312	5	299	13401	22	1827	22512	15	942	14127	5	319	998	1	74
1923	6121	3	546	14311	6	888	27813	23	3797	13060	13	1690	25405	6	945	1539	1	188
1924	7228	3	540	16967	6	817	41543	23	3631	12494	13	1656	31599	6	890	1537	1	173
1925	6349	3	535	18777	6	735	44954	22	3731	13181	12	1690	43241	6	880	1995	1	180
1926	5041	3	532	18434	6	716	41104	23	3753	11956	12	1678	43708	6	880	1611	1	180
1927	7411	3	546	22186	5	721	47268	23	3723	13713	12	1748	47925	6	952	1976	1	193
1928	5821	3	552	22490	5	736	39917	23	3792	12425	12	1647	43480	7	1018	1838	1	230
1929	6325	3	531	19248	5	723	32762	23	3757	11583	12	1682	47160	7	1035	1808	1	172
1930	7384	3	539	20815	5	712	31116	20	3535	10825	11	1630	45133	7	1068	1578	1	169
1931	6559	3	529	18892	5	699	32582	20	3256	9969	11	1510	49729	7	1054	1517	1	172
1932	5579	3	526	15667	5	688	20282	19	3216	8039	10	1444	48963	7	1062	958	1	171
1933	6457	3	530	13630	4	647	42457	19	3068	7670	10	1376	37777	6	1004	503	1	170

*Official GWR statistics state that Wanstrow station did not open until April 1909 (see text)

the branch, Yatton station is still in regular use, but Witham station has vanished completely. Very little of the Yatton - Cranmore section has been built over, the only conspicuous redevelopment being that of the section at Axbridge, which is now incorporated in a revised alignment of the A371. Frustratingly, though, the route does not offer too much scope for lengthy walks.

Contributor's note: Sincere thanks are due to Messrs. Eric Youldon, Bill Peto and Bryan Wilson for their invaluable assistance during the preparation of this article.

Above : More of the Coronation Garden at Yatton, 25th May 1953. PHOTOGRAPH R.C. RILEY.

Hi de hi! Ex-GWR clerestory coach 9902 ultimately found a new home - and a new purpose - at Cheddar. The date is 24th August 1956. A camping coach was kept at Cheddar from 1934 until 1962 inclusive and the vehicles were also available - at various times - at Axbridge, Congresbury, Wells and Wookey. The Axbridge and Wookey coaches were dispensed with by the early 1950s (if not before), but coaches remained at Congresbury and Wells until 1963. The last summer of camping coach operation on the WR was 1964. PHOTOGRAPH R.M. CASSERLEY.